𝒟

INTERESTING WAYS TO TEACH

53 Interesting Ways to Assess Your Students

53 Interesting Ways to Assess Your Students

Sue Habeshaw

Senior Lecturer and Course Adviser
University of the West of England, Bristol

Graham Gibbs

Professor and Director,
Centre for Higher Education Practice
The Open University

Trevor Habeshaw

Educational Consultant
TES Associates, Bristol

First published in 1986 by
Technical and Educational Services Ltd.
37 Ravenswood Road
Bristol BS6 6BW
U.K.

Revised Edition 1993
Reprinted 1995, 1998

ISBN 0 947885 12 9

Printed in Great Britain by
The Cromwell Press Ltd,
Aintree Avenue, White Horse Business Park
Trowbridge, Wiltshire BA14 0XB U.K.

Distributed by
Plymbridge Distributors Ltd,
Estover Rd.,
Plymouth PL6 7PZ
telephone   +44 (0) 1752) 202301
fax   +44 (0) 1752) 202333
email   *orders@plymbridge.com*
website   *https://www.plymbridge.com*

All books published by TES Ltd. can be browsed and ordered from our website
http://www.web-direct.co.uk/tes

Books from Technical & Educational Services

The 53 series
53 Interesting things to do in your lectures
53 Interesting things to do in your seminars and tutorials
53 Interesting ways to assess your students
53 Interesting ways of helping your students to study
53 Interesting communication exercises for science students
53 Interesting ways to appraise your teaching
53 Interesting ways to promote equal opportunities in education
53 Interesting ways to teach mathematics
53 Interesting ways to ask questios in mathematics and statistics
53 Interesting ways to write open learning materials
53 Interesting activities for open learning courses
53 Problems with large classes: *Making the best of a bad job*
53 Questions and answers about modules and semesters
53 Interesting ways to supervise student projects, dissertations & theses

Interesting ways to teach
Preparing to teach: *An introduction to effective teaching in higher education*
253 Ideas for your teaching
Interesting ways to teach: *12 Do-it-yourself staff development exercises*
Creating a teaching profile

Other titles
Getting the most from your data: *Practical ideas on how to analyse qualitative data*
Writing study guides
Improving the quality of student learning
HMA Stationery Ltd. *(an open & flexible learning study pack)*

Acknowledgements

We wish to thank these friends for their help and support
in the publication of this book

Jo Corke

Jenny Walters

Preface to the first edition

This book is addressed to teachers in further and higher education, though it is probably equally suitable for nurse tutors, YTS trainers, and others. Teachers in schools, too, will be able to adapt these ideas to their own situations.

The purpose of this book is to describe a wide range of ways of assessing students and to encourage teachers to extend the repertoire of assessment methods that they use. Variety is an important factor in effective assessment, as in effective teaching, and choice enables teachers to select those assessment methods which support their educational aims.

Though each item is written to make sense on its own, groups of items are gathered together under broader headings, and cross referenced, so that comparisons can easily be made. The methods range from the familiar standard essay to more technical areas such as computer based assessment and unconventional areas such as alternative exams.

Assessment is an aspect of education which, understandably, tends to raise student anxiety. When introducing a new method of assessment, you can help your students by telling them what it involves, explaining why you think it is worth doing and giving them time to think about it and discuss it.

Bristol 1986

Preface to the third edition

This book was the third in the series *Interesting Ways to Teach*. Since it was first written ten *53* books and a number of other books of direct relevance to teachers in further and higher education have been added as TES has expanded its list.

The book has been substantially revised in order to include some more contemporary aspects of assessment in higher education. In particular, two new chapters have been added: *Involving students in the assessment process* and *Issues in assessment.*

Bristol 1993

Contents   Page

Chapter 11 Issues in assessment

Chapter 1
Essays

1 Standard essay

2 Role play essay

3 Structured essay

4 Interpretation of evidence

5 Design

6 Note-form essay

7 Hypothesis formation

Standard essay 1

Essay questions are probably used for coursework and final exams more frequently than any other type of assessment. There are characteristic problems, and advantages, associated with different types of essay question. Different types are suitable for assessing different aspects of student learning and different course objectives. Popular varieties of standard essay include the following:

Quotation: Discuss (or Comment, or Query)

Q. 'Land values are both a product and a determinant of the pattern of urban development.' Discuss (see note1).

Q. Comment on the assertion that 'although a good case can be made for free trade on the grounds of economic efficiency, there is no case on the grounds of equity'.

Q. 'Even after Locke's book was written the subject remained almost untouched and I fear that I will leave it pretty much as I found it' (Rousseau: the Preface to *Emile*). Did Rousseau leave education as he found it?

If the quotation is being used to encourage students to challenge expert opinion, this type of question can be helpful. If, however, its purpose is mainly decorative, then students will have problems working out what is important about the quotation. Obscure and invented quotations are likely to cause both students and markers considerable difficulties and confuse the issue as to what ability or knowledge is actually being assessed.

Write an essay on . . .

Q. Write an essay on fluid mechanics.

Q. Write an essay on language development in Down's Syndrome children up to 5 years.

Such questions run a variety of risks:

*   The open-endedness makes it easy for students to cobble together enough disconnected facts and ideas to pass without revealing much thought or understanding.

*   When they are used in examinations, students can revise and prepare complete answers on likely topics and trot them out without thought or reformulation.

*   Students can be stalled and panicked by the scope offered them.

*   Students may be being asked to produce an answer of a greater degree of generality than ever before.

*   It isn't at all clear what would count as an acceptable answer.

Questions of this form may simply reveal their authors' inability to clarify their own teaching goals or their inablity to translate these into clear questions.

The potential advantage of such questions is the freedom it gives to students to choose what they will concentrate on and to structure their work themselves. This may allow excellent students to stand out more. However it may also give weaker students plenty of rope with which to hang themselves.

Describe, Give an account of, Compare, Contrast, Explain

Q. Describe how the Monte Carlo technique is used to shed light on the small sample properties of various estimation techniques.

Q. Give an account of the discovery and early use of penicillin.

Q. Compare and contrast the foreign policies of Disraeli and Gladstone.

Q. Explain the Phillips Curve and its applications.

Unlike 'Assess. . .' questions, these questions do not explicitly require the student to express a viewpoint or conclusion. If there is such a requirement it should be clearly stated and the key issues specified, e.g.

Q. Give an account of the discovery and early use of penicillin. What is your view of the scientific significance of this early work?

Q. Compare and contrast the foreign policies of Disraeli and Gladstone. Who was more successful, in your view, in protecting Britain's overseas interests? Justify your view with reference to events outside Europe.

Assess, Analyse, Evaluate

Q. Assess Richard as a strategist in the light of the expedition to Ireland in 1394.

Q. Analyse the difference between Locke's and Froebel's use of play in the education of young children.

Q. Evaluate the contribution of Japanese prints to the development of Impressionism.

These questions require not just information from the student, but a reasoned conclusion.

Trick questions

Q. Is literalism a symptom of a dose of Flew?

Q. Can you do two things at once?

Q. Who, or what, unbound Prometheus?

While these questions may be very clever, they are probably only under-stood by the people who set them and their favourite students. The first is from an English literature paper, the second from a cognitive psychology paper, and the third is from an 18th century English history course and refers to the Industrial Revolution. Only those who attended all the lectures and the right seminars could have a clue what was being referred to. Trick questions are not recommended.

Note 1   A version of this question, from town planning, is used in each item of this chapter so as to illustrate the way a question can be developed to assess different objectives and channel students' efforts in different ways.

Role play essay 2

Q. You have inherited your late uncle's urban estate under his will and are considering whether it would be more profitable to sell the property quickly or 'sit and speculate'. Describe some of the factors you would consider in making your decision.

Q. Write a letter to the Minister of Education protesting about the lack of nursery school places in your county, giving economic arguments and emphasising evidence in government reports.

Q. Imagine you are a French journalist working for *Le Monde*. Write an article for the politics page about Britain's attitude towards trade in agricultural produce within the EEC, with specific reference to recent incidents involving French agricultural produce.

Such questions help students to see the relevance of the task and to take a personal interest in it. Their writing often becomes more natural and fluent. Even very small elements of simulation or role play can dramatically change students' approach to questions. There is of course a danger of encouraging too flippant an approach but this can be kept in check by careful phrasing of the question, e.g. get students to write for *The Times* rather than the *Sun* or write to their member of parliament, not to a friend.

This type of question is often used in law and accountancy with the instructions: 'Advise your client . . .' The same kind of instructions can be given in any subject area, e.g.

Q. Advise Weybridge Electrical Ltd. (by whom you have been hired as a consultant) on the suitability of the circuit designs in Appendix I given the performance specifications in Appendix II.

Q. Prepare a parliamentary answer for the Chancellor of the Exchequer (of whose think tank on the economy you are a prominent member) to the following tabled question concerning the recently published inflation figures: . . . .

Advise him on likely supplementary questions and on appropriate answers.

Structured essay 3

Q. Identify and discuss some of the determinants of urban land values
and their impact on urban development. In your answer you should:

a define the following terms:
   property rights in land,
   zoning,
   site value rating;

b explain the influence of these terms in determining land values;

c select one activity of public authorities, and one market factor,
   which affect land values and explain how each might influence
   urban development.

Q. Undertake a stylistic analysis of the following passage. Select, arrange
and comment on features of syntax, lexis, semantics and (where
relevant) phonology. Relate the artistic effects of the passage to the
writer's choice of language.

By specifying the content in this way it is possible, when marking, to be
clearer whether students know about and understand the specific things
which you think are important. At the same time it becomes difficult to tell
whether students would know which things are important without such
prompting. You have to decide whether it is specific knowledge and
techniques, or the ability to identify what is important, which is what you
want to assess.

Questions can also be written in such a way that they specify the structure
of the essay, e.g.

Q. Is *Heart of Darkness* a Victorian novel?

Discuss the characteristic features of Victorian novels. Identify the key differences of post-Victorian novels. Highlight the main characteristics of *Heart of Darkness*. On the basis of the preceding three sections, draw conclusions about the extent to which *Heart of Darkness* is a Victorian novel.

Again you have to decide whether it is students' subject knowledge and analytical skills which you want to assess, or their ability to structure their own essays. If it is the former, then this type of question, by giving them a structure to use, will enable them to concentrate on content.

Interpretation of evidence 4

Q. You own a house in a developing suburban area but are considering selling your property and moving closer to the city centre. Given the following demographic data:

....

....

what economic and social factors would you consider in coming to a decision?

Q. What light does the following experimental evidence throw on Triesman's model of selective attention?

....

....

Many standard essay questions (see item 1) rely on students having undertaken analysis and interpretation at an earlier stage, e.g. before an exam, and simply recalling these analyses in their answers. Interpretation questions require students to undertake this analysis 'live', and this can prevent regurgitation.

Design   5

Q. Design a new small shopping precinct for the site below . . . .

To the above design brief can be added a requirement for the interpretation of evidence:

Q. Given the street plans, existing locations of shops, site values and other information in Appendices A–D, design and site a new small shopping precinct.

To this can be added elements of role play and structured questions:

Q. You are involved with the design of a new small shopping precinct. Given the street plans, existing locations of shops, site values and other information in Appendices A - D, draft an outline design for, and site, a new small shopping precinct which involves the demolition of an old street. Consider the possible effects on land value and accessibility of such a redevelopment and present an argument for such a siting to the planning officer.

This last version of the design question emphasises a quite different aspect of the design process and illustrates the way structured questions can focus on specific issues.

Design questions are common in architecture and town planning. They are not so common in a number of other subject areas where they are just as appropriate. For example in scientific and technical subjects the skills of experimental design are usually taught and assessed through teacher-designed experiments. It may not be until final-year undergraduate work, or even postgraduate work, that students design their own experiments. Even then less time tends to be spent on the design stage than on executing the design. Similarly in craft subjects, planning out how to undertake a complex task is often not tackled until late on in courses when all the component skills have been mastered.

It is easy to set design tasks (as in architecture) in order to develop the design skills required, even when the skills necessary to implement the design have not yet been acquired, and there is no intention of implementing the design, e.g.

Q. Design a method for establishing the frequency of occurrence of a particular microfossil in a sample of shale.

Q. Design an experiment to test the duration of short-term memory for verbal items following different kinds of initial information processing.

Note-form essay 6

Q. List the main economic factors which affect the pattern of changing land values. For each factor, itemise its limitations and potentialities for predicting future urban development. Your answer may be in note form.

Q. Briefly describe the significance for oil exploration of each of the following microfossil types:

....

....

etc.

This type of question is used most often to assess the recall of key items of information or test simple understanding of terms, formulae, apparatus, tools and so on. It is less suitable for assessing analysis, synthesis of ideas, creativity and so on. Sometimes note-form questions are used to assess whether students understand what is significant about a topic, e.g.

Q. Write notes on two of the following:
   a   ....
   b   ....
   c   ....
   d   ....

Students who have plenty to say about the topics and are obliged to select the main points are faced with the problem of guessing which aspects the marker thinks are most important. Poor students can gain marks by writing down whatever comes into their heads about any of the topics, and this may be why this form of question is so common: to avoid having to fail very poor students. Note-form essays are also easier and quicker (though less interesting) to mark.

Hypothesis formation 7

Q. Suggest the relationship between nearby house prices and:

   a   the development of a new shopping precinct in a suburban area;
   b   a road-widening scheme in the same area.

Hypothesis formation questions can be combined with data interpretation to encourage students to be speculative in their analyses:

Q. Speculate as to the possible causes of the data trends in the table below:
   . . . . . .

or linked to design questions to encourage self-criticism or reflection. For example the question developed in item 5 above ('Design a new small shopping precinct for the site below . . . . . .') could be expanded by the addition of the question:

Q. Speculate as to the likely planning objections raised to your plans by:

   a   the local community;
   b   the planning officer.

Chapter 2

Objective tests

Using objective tests to assess knowledge   8

Objective tests are tests which produce student answers (or responses, or actions, or products) which can be marked objectively. Requiring someone to clear five feet in the high jump is an objective test, for example: everyone would agree whether or not the person had failed the jump. Simple factual tests are also usually objective tests. For example, marking answers to the question 'What is the capital of Canada?' involves little in the way of subjective judgement (except perhaps in the matter of spelling mistakes, and even these judgements could be made objective by specifying in advance which spelling mistakes would be tolerated). An essay is not an objective test because its requirements cannot be specified sufficiently clearly to allow objective marking.

Objective tests have a number of potential advantages.
*   They can be marked quickly. This is especially the case when students indicate their answers by ticking possible alternatives as with multiple choice questions.

*   They can be highly reliable. In particular, where a team of tutors is involved, objective tests ensure that all tutors are marking to the same standard.

*   They can be marked easily. This can allow either less experienced tutors (for example post-graduates or 3rd year undergraduates), students' peers or even computers (see item 11) to mark student work.

Quick, reliable and easy marking allows a greater proportion of a syllabus to be tested than is possible with assessment methods (such as essay marking) which are slow, unreliable and difficult to mark. This can provide a much better overall indication of a student's achievement on a course than the very narrow sampling achieved by more time-consuming methods.

Objective tests are particularly useful as one component of overall assessment systems, achieving some of the aims of a course very economically and allowing more resources to be allocated to other more demanding forms of assessment. They also have the effect of focusing students' attention on some basic features of the content of the course which might otherwise slip past unnoticed.

The simpler forms of objective test can be used to assess students' knowledge and understanding. Types of questions include:

Right/Wrong (or True/False).
Students have to indicate whether a statement is right or wrong.

Q. The First Lord of the Treasury is the Chancellor of the Exchequer.
    True/False

True/false questions are open to guessing. Random choice would score 50% and sensible guessing more than 50%. A simple guessing correction can be made by subtracting the number of questions answered incorrectly from the total answered correctly to give the score.

Short answer (or Completion)
Students have only a small space - perhaps enough for a short sentence - to answer a question. Short answer questions may also take the form of short lists, as in: 'State the three main causes of ...' It can be helpful to indicate the length of answer required by use of dotted lines or spaces in the layout:

Q. What were the three recommendations of the Trevelyan Report of 1854?
    1 ....
    2 ....
    3 ....

Completion questions consist of an incomplete statement which the student must finish.

Q. The standard deviation can be derived from a normal distribution curve by dropping a perpendicular line from the .... to cut the .... axis.

Questions of this type can be used as the first section of a conventional exam.

Matching
Students have to match items in one list with items in a second list. (It is advisable to have more items in the second list than in the first to prevent the last match being made by elimination.)

Q. Match each of the items in List X with one of the dates in List Y by filling in the boxes below the lists. Do not use any of the dates in List Y more than once.

List X	List Y
1 County Borough Councils set up	A 1894
2 Urban District Councils set up	B 1895
3 County Councils set up	C 1902
4 Educational duties transferred from School Boards to Councils	D 1929 E 1888
5 Powers of Boards of Guardians transferred to Councils	F 1835

List X	1	2	3	4	5
List Y					

Multiple choice

This is perhaps the most common form of objective test. Students have to identify the correct answer from a short list of alternatives.

Q. A customs tax is imposed on Japanese toys imported into the United Kingdom in order to give direct assistance to:
   a   UK importers
   b   UK exporters
   c   Japanese toymakers
   d   UK toymakers
   e   Japanese exporters

For suggestions about the use of objective tests to assess higher order learning outcomes, see item 9.

Using objective tests to assess more than just knowledge　9

Objective tests are most commonly used to assess knowledge (see item 8). It is, however, possible to devise objective tests which assess comprehension, application, analysis, synthesis, computation, interpretation and reasoning and yet which are still easily marked.

Tests of this kind can provide students with more frequent feedback than is possible with other kinds of assessment. (In addition to the test scores, standard feedback comments can be produced to explain the answers.) Students can use this information to help them decide what further work they need to do. This is a process commonly used in the Keller Plan and Teach-Test methods.

The tests provide tutors with information on the progress of the whole class so that they can make informed decisions about the focus of remedial lectures, follow-up tutorials or problem sessions. They also enable tutors to target remedial and specialist help on those students who need it.

The simpler forms of objective test can be adapted to test higher order learning outcomes, for example:

Q. What is the square root of 169?

Q. Given the above case study and data, which of the following statements about the situation are true?
　1　'.......................'　True/False
　2　'.......................'　True/False
　3　etc.

Q. Given the following series of shoe sizes:
　4, 4, 4, 5, 6, 9, 10

which number gives the median?

A	4
B	5
C	6
D	9
E	10

Which number gives the mode?

A	4
B	5
C	6
D	9
E	10

Other forms of objective test lend themselves more readily to higher order learning outcomes. Types of question include:

Multiple completion
Instead of selecting a single correct answer, as with multiple choice questions, students have to select the only correct combination from a list of combinations of answers.

Q. The assets of a commercial bank can be set out in the following categories:

1 Investments
2 Bills discounted
3 Money at call and short notice
4 Advances
5 Cash in hand and at the Bank of England

Which of the following combinations of the above assets comprises the liquidity ratio?

A 1, 2 and 3
B 2 and 3

C   2, 3 and 4
D   2, 3 and 5
E   3, 4 and 5

Assertion/Reason
Here the question is set out in the form of an assertion or statement, and a reason or explanation of it. The student must decide whether the assertion and reason are correct statements, and whether the reason adequately explains the assertion.

Q.	Assertion	Reason
	The monarch rules Britain	The law assumes that the monarch can do no wrong

Tick A, B, C, D or E
A   The assertion and reason are correct statements AND the reason correctly explains the assertion.
B   The assertion and reason are correct statements BUT the reason does not explain the assertion.
C   The assertion is correct BUT the reason is incorrect.
D   The assertion is incorrect BUT the reason is correct.
E   BOTH the assertion and reason are incorrect.

(The answer to this question is D.)

This format looks complex and confusing at first, but with familiarity it can be used to test reasoning as well as recall and comprehension. It can also be used in conjunction with a case study, experimental evidence, data etc. to test students' interpretation of the evidence, as in the next question.

Q.   Given the above statistics concerning law and order, and crimes committed between 1950 and 1990, code each of the following pairs of statements and explanations, using the A - E answer codes given above:

Answer

Code	Statement	Explanation
1	Murders increased between 1970 and 1990.	There were fewer police per 1,000 of the population.
2	etc............	

Best Answer

Best answer questions tend to be more difficult than other types of objective test. They involve finer discriminations and wrong answers are not so obviously wrong that they are easy to eliminate. Best answer questions can be useful when an understanding or interpretation of information is required and can be used following data or case studies.

Q. A manual for an aptitude test reports a Kuder-Richardson reliability of +0.95 for 25,000 children. Which of the following conclusions about the test is most appropriate?

> A It is highly reliable
> B It is highly valid
> C It is highly internally consistent
> D It is suitable for selection purposes

Chapter 3

Computer-based assessment

Computer-generated assignments 10

With the help of the computer you can devise assignments for your students which are varied, plentiful and very speedily produced.

Computer-generated test papers
Sometimes it is necessary to have alternative versions of a test paper of equal difficulty: for resits, for subsequent years, to prevent students from helping one another (should that be considered undesirable), and so on. With some forms of objective test item it is a very simple matter to produce alternative versions of an item with only minor changes of wording or content, e.g.

Q. A1   Give the electronic configuration of the following ions:
             Fe(II)   Cu(II)   Ni(II) *or*
    A2   Give the electronic configuration of the following ions:
             Fe(III)   Ti(III)   Ni(III)

Q. B1   Draw the orbitals:
             dyz   dxz *or*
    B2   Draw the orbitals:
             dxz   dxz-yz

These alternative items for each topic can then be typed into a file in a computer:

Topic area	A	B	C	D	etc.
Item	A1	B1	C1	D1	etc.
	A2	B2	C2	D2	etc.
	A3	B3	C3	D3	etc.
	A4	etc	. . .	. . .	. . .

A simple programme will randomly select one item from topic area A, one from topic area B, and so on, and print out the resulting list of items. In this way a unique test paper can be printed for each student.

Computer-generated problems

In most science and technology subjects students are required to do problems involving calculations with answers which are either right or wrong. Usually the tutor demonstrates how to do a particular kind of problem and then sets the students a couple of examples to try for themselves. A difficulty for the tutor is that there is a limit to the number of problems which it is practical to set: it simply takes too long to devise a large number of comparable problems and to calculate the correct numerical answers in order to be able to mark students' work. Individual students don't get as much practice as might be desirable, and it becomes very easy for students to collaborate or cheat because they are all tackling the same problems and can easily check their answers with one another.

It is relatively easy to produce a computer program which generates unique problems, allowing students to get as much practice as they need, preventing unwanted collaboration, and calculating correct answers to aid marking.

One version of such a program has the following components:

a   a file containing the names of the students in the class for whom problems are to be generated

b   a question in a specified format

c   an algorithm for calculating the correct answer from the variables in the question

d   a file containing a set of permissible values for each variable e   a tutor's file in which are stored the values generated for each of the variables for each student, and the answer to each problem, calculated from the algorithm.

The questions can be of the following form (the variables are italicised).

Q. If *six 20 horsepower* pumps can empty *three 10,000 ton* oil tankers in *24 hours* how long will it take to empty *two 8,000 ton* tankers with *four 30 horsepower* pumps?

There are 4 variables in this question and if 5 permissible values were input for each variable it would be possible to generate $5^4 = 625$ unique problems by randomly selecting one of the permissible values for each of the variables. The program will print out a sheet for each student with the student's name on it and a unique problem, and will record on a file for the tutor the values involved (in this case: 6, 20, 3, 10,000, 24, 2, 8,000, 4, and 30) and the correct answer, calculated with the algorithm. Marking then simply involves checking students' answers against those in the tutor's file. Automatic marking could be added to this program (see item 11) and tutorial comments for incorrect answers could be given automatically by inserting the student's unique values for the variables into a standard explanation of how to do the calculation (see item 12).

Words, or letter strings, can be substituted for numerical data as variables in questions, to allow the use of this question generator in subject areas not involving numerical calculations. However this is likely to be more difficult than for numerical applications.

Once the program has been written, you only need to specify the question format, the algorithm, and the names of the students, to be able to generate as many problems as you need, together with their answers.

Computer marking 11

Objective tests which involve students selecting alternative answers by ticking boxes can be marked by computer, thus saving marking time. Computer marking can be undertaken in two main ways.

Optical Mark Reader (OMR)
The OMR is a device attached to a computer which can recognise the position of graphite marks on standard pre-printed forms. Students indicate their answers to questions by marking boxes on the forms in pencil. The answer forms are then automatically read by the OMR and results are stored on the computer. Standard software usually provides class results for the tutor, results of individual students showing which answers were correct, and an analysis of the pattern of responses to each question to help the tutor identify questions which were misleading or ambiguous or too easy or too hard. The simplest and most useful systems involve separating the question sheets from the answer sheets, so that standard answer sheets can be used for all tests and standard analysis software can be used without modification for each test. Questions may be displayed on an overhead projector where students are undertaking the test in a lecture theatre, or on printed test papers under examination conditions.

Once an OMR has been set up, for example as a data preparation service in a computer centre, it is easy for tutors to use it for a variety of marking purposes, and to mark frequently. If the service has a fast turn-round time (for example it is 12 hours at Oxford Brookes University) this enables tutors to give students rapid feedback and to make immediate teaching decisions based on student performance.

On-screen testing
Software such as QUESTION MARK allows questions to be posed on the computer screen and students to answer them by pressing keys. The

responses are stored and collated automatically. Tutors can write banks of test items and students can select sets of questions at an appropriate level or be tested by the tutor from random selections of questions at a particular level. (This ensures that each student is tested with a different set of items to prevent copying.)

Such systems are easy to operate, use no paper and provide students with instant feedback. They do require tutor time to set up the questions and they entail the use of one terminal or micro per student, though all students do not need to take the test at the same time. Because of the difficulty of preventing students from helping one another when working at terminals or micros, on-screen testing is more appropriately used for providing feedback on learning than for generating course marks.

Reference
G Gibbs, *Using the Optical Mark Reader 2: Marking Multiple Choice Tests*, Educational Methods Unit, Oxford Polytechnic, 1987.

Computer-based feedback to students 12

With computer-marked assessment the only feedback students usually get is a score for the number of correct answers. Even in the Open University, which pioneered the widescale use of computer marked tests and undertakes very sophisticated analysis and development of the tests themselves, until recently the only information that students were given about their assignment was their grade (i.e. A, B, C etc). They had no way of knowing which questions they got wrong, or why.

As feedback is so important to learning it is worth thinking about how to provide feedback even within a computer-based assessment system. The system described here is known as T.I.P.S. (Teaching Information Processing System). This is a system developed at Duke University, U.S.A., and adapted for the assessment of economics students at Heriot Watt University, Edinburgh, and of science students at the University of Ulster.

When writing the test items, the author also writes a tutorial comment which would provide the basis for answering the item correctly. When the computer marks a student's responses to the assessment questions it also prints out a total score, and the tutorial comments for the questions which the student answered incorrectly, e.g.

Student progress report

Student　　　　　　　A.N. Other

Survey No.　　　　　1

Biochemistry Test No.　3

You correctly answered 23 out of the 25 questions in this survey.

Amides are generally neutral. The carbonyl removes the basic properties from the adjacent -NH2 or -NHR.

Oxidation of a mercapton (thiol), RSH, causes two molecules to link to give a disulphide RSSR and water is eliminated.

Reference
J. D. Ruddick, 'The Use of T.I.P.S. with Physiotherapy Students' in G. Gibbs (Ed), *Alternatives in Assessment 2: Objective Tests and Computer Applications*, Standing Conference on Educational Development Services in Polytechnics, Occasional Paper 21, Birmingham, 1985.

Computer-managed assessment 13

As well as generating assessment material for students and acting as testing devices, computers can be used in various ways as administrative aids.

Assessment record keeping
With large numbers of students taking large numbers of tests it can be valuable to have an automated record keeping system to keep track of individual student progress, and identify those who have not completed many tests or who regularly take several attempts to pass. The records can also be used to review the assessment tests themselves. Software such as QUESTION MARK (see item 11) can be backed up by data bases of results for each student and results for each item of a test.

Weighting
The use of spreadsheets allows the easy handling of different weightings for different assessment elements and other rubrics which staff may have devised for calculating overall assessment grades.

Monitoring and evaluation
The results stored on the computer provide the raw data from which can be obtained a range of kinds of information for use in the monitoring and evaluation of courses:

• the percentage of students in each degree class each year, broken down by gender, entry qualifications, ethnic origin, disability etc.

• the non-progression rate each year, with percentages of students withdrawing, deferring or failing

• the mean and standard deviation of the marks for each module or section of the course

- the mean and standard deviation of the marks for each type of assessment on a course.

Computerised data of this kind can be set against annual student and staff evaluations and external examiners' reports to maintain an ongoing record of the history of a course. It can also be used to gauge the effects on a course of such factors as increasing student numbers and a decreasing unit of resource. At Oxford Brookes University such data from the modular degree has been stored on the computer since 1981 and used in studies of this kind.

Assessed computer simulations   **14**

Computers are used increasingly to provide sophisticated simulations of events or phenomena beyond the normal scope of conventional study: simulations of the British economy, simulations of the ecological state of a lake, simulations of human physiological functioning, simulations of the performance of a retail outlet etc. Such simulations are frequently used in teaching, mainly as demonstrations. Students' understanding of the systems and concepts upon which the simulations are based is then usually assessed in a conventional way: by a written exam, for example. However there are a variety of ways of designing assessment directly around the use of computer simulations.

Manchester University Medical School has produced sophisticated simulations of various aspects of human functioning for training and research purposes. They are often used in biology departments to illustrate the biochemical processes involved in, for example, respiration. One such simulation, 'MACPUFF', allows the user to 'set up' a simulated patient with a chosen set of respiratory variables, in a particular atmospheric environment, and then 'run' the patient for several minutes to see what happens to various vital indicators of health and physiological functioning. Biochemical measures are calculated, listed every three seconds and plotted on graphs, and it is possible to observe the complex patterns of chemical interactions involved in maintaining a stable and healthy respiratory state.

Students' understanding of these interactions can be assessed if, for example, instructions are given to set the 'patient' up in a particular way, and then to manipulate variables (such as the amount of oxygen in the air supply) in order to stabilise the patient's condition. A full record of all interventions, and the exact consequences of these, is made automatically. A criterion referenced assessment (see item 38) could include the requirement to stabilise the patient's condition within certain parameters, and within a time limit. Such a goal cannot be achieved by trial and error, but only through an understanding of the biochemistry of respiration. The student might take many hours reading, devising intervention strategies, and then trying these out on the simulation. At the end the student would simply hand in the print-out recording the successful stabilisation of the patient, or keep a full print-out including all the unsuccessful interventions for later discussion.

Computer simulations of the economy are commonplace in economics teaching. They are normally used as an illustration or perhaps as a game. But they can also be used in the same way as in the MACPUFF example above. A desired economic state for five years' hence can be specified and today's economic indicators input at the start. Students can then be set the task of achieving this desired state by manipulating those economic variables within the control of, say, the Chancellor of the Exchequer. Students can also be required to provide a commentary on the computer print-out of their economic performance, so as to demonstrate their understanding of the logic of the interaction of the variables they have manipulated.

The teaching of accountancy and financial management on computers often involves sample data in accounts software packages, and can include other elements of simulation such as company names and records of past dealings. Such material can be used as the basis of assessment tasks. For example :

Q.   Mr. Jones of Toltrek Ltd has an appointment with you in one hour to discuss dealings with your firm since 1 April of this year. From the database you have, prepare and print out the financial information you will require at this meeting.

Such a task has the added advantage of being similar to the real world tasks which the student is being trained to undertake.

Computer-marked practicals 15

Practicals in science and technology often have as their main aims to get students to take accurate measurements and obtain accurate results, and to get students to make correct calculations using the correct mathematical procedures.

This causes problems for the marker. It is often not possible to tell how accurate an individual student's results are, given the errors that arise from the laboratory equipment, conditions, samples etc. Only gross inaccuracies tend to be noticed and reflected in marks, and there is no real incentive for the students to be very careful and accurate in their laboratory methods. In addition, to check every student's calculations by hand can be very tedious and time consuming, and again it is common for only gross errors or the use of incorrect formulae to be spotted and reflected in marks. Finally, by the time students get their marked reports back it is too late to do anything about rectifying mistakes or inaccuracies, even if the students still cared about the practical. The effort students put into writing up their reports and the time tutors spend marking them does not seem to lead to improvements in accuracy and technique in quantitative laboratory work.

These problems can be addressed by the use of a computer to check on the accuracy of students' results and calculations and to give them immediate feedback during the practical. To illustrate how this can be done an example of a chemistry-based computer assessment program is described.

On completing the practical students go to a micro on which the appropriate program is already running. They enter their names. They are then asked a series of questions, e.g.

Q. What mass of sodium oxalate did you use? (in grams)

Students enter all the relevant data in response to these questions. Then questions are posed which require calculations and quantitative conclusions from the data, e.g.

Q. What is the concentration of the sodium tetraborate in solution? (in moles/litre)

The program calculates what the correct answers to these questions should be, given each student's own data, and compares its own answers to those of the student, displaying feedback such as :

Your answer to question 1
'What is the concentration of the sodium tetraborate in solution?'
was *wrong*.
You have had 1 attempt.

The program awards marks for correct answers (and fewer marks if students take several attempts) and keeps track of total marks. If the purpose of the experiment is to establish a standard value, marks are awarded to students according to how close their results come to the class mean. An individual's result which was the same as the class mean would get full marks, and results different from the mean would get proportionately fewer marks according to how many standard deviations away from the mean their results were, with a result over 4 standard deviations away getting zero.

The list of class results with their mean and standard deviation, and each individual's consequent mark, can be printed out and displayed as soon as all students have entered their data onto the micro, before the end of the practical. In this way students get immediate feedback on their performance. This has a marked effect on the care they take in their laboratory techniques and on the overall accuracy of their results. They do their calculations during the practical instead of afterwards and they have the opportunity of correcting their mistakes. A great deal of time is saved as well: students do not have to write up laboratory reports, and the tutor does

does not have to mark them.

Although each chemistry experiment requires a unique program which specifies the correct values and undertakes the correct calculations, the unique elements of the program are short and simple to write. The common elements and the basic framework for eliciting students' data and allocating and recording their marks represent the major part of the program and can easily be adapted to a variety of different quantitative experiments in any subject area in only about 15 minutes.

The program for the chemistry practicals described here can be obtained from:

Dr. Peter Grebenik
Department of Geology and Physical Sciences
Oxford Brookes University
Oxford OX3 0BP
U.K.

Chapter 4

Exams

Standard exam   **16**

The standard exam - a three-hour unseen paper with limited choice - remains a popular mode of assessment, in spite of the rival attractions of continuous assessment and alternative exams. There are various reasons for this. Some course teams are obliged to assess their students with a standard exam because of the requirements of professional bodies. Other course teams find that the standard exam is the best response to an increase in student numbers: it eases the marking load and ensures that students do not copy one another's work. Yet others use the standard exam because they have found ways of making it work for their courses. And students themselves, though they generally find exams stressful, will often say that it was only when they were revising for an unseen exam that the course really came together for them and made sense as a whole.

If an exam is to be an appropriate assessment, it must be based on the objectives of the course. You will need to decide whether you want to test students' ability simply to memorise material, or to understand it, or in addition to apply, analyse, synthesise or evaluate it. Set your questions accordingly, being sure to use specific instructions such as 'describe', 'explain' or 'assess'. If your students' exams are set by outside bodies, you can identify their requirements by checking out the examiners' reports and exam questions from previous years.

You can help your students to be clear about what is required of them by holding revision sessions in which you work through sample papers with them and show them how to tackle the questions in the time allowed. Mock exams in strictly timed conditions will reinforce this learning and also by habituating students to the process will make the exam itself less stressful.

Seen exam 17

It could be argued that conventional three-hour unseen exams, with no access to books, notes or other resources, are a rather curious way of testing ability. Students will probably never face the same kind of test under such extreme time pressure in any subsequent work. Exams even bear little resemblance to independent postgraduate research. A more realistic way of testing students would assess their ability to research, use resources, draft and redraft.

Seen exams, in which students are given copies of the exam paper prior to the exam, test these abilities. They also eliminate the element of luck involved in question spotting. Students are less anxious about the exam and their answers are of a higher quality. This type of exam is popular because it is seen to offer the advantages of both exams and coursework. It does, however, also have some disadvantages: it is disruptive of other courses or exams; it puts a lot of pressure on library provision, though this can be minimised by placing crucial books on very short loan; and there is of course an increased likelihood of cheating because students are able to get outside help. If this is a problem for you, you can intersperse your seen exams with enough unseen exams to act as a check on them.

There are two main types of seen exam.

The nine-month exam
If you give students copies of the exam paper at the beginning of the course, this will act as a course map, indicating to them which parts of it are important and which are peripheral. The main problem with the nine-month exam is that students may orient themselves narrowly to the exam questions and take unexamined topics less seriously during the course. This can be minimised by setting broad and theoretical questions which have no right answers and which require considerable thought rather than mere reproduction.

Another problem is that students may memorise whole answers. The exam can become an exercise in writing out from memory an answer prepared some time before, though this may not matter much provided that the original learning has been undertaken.

The one-week exam

The one-week exam involves giving students copies of the exam paper one week before the exam date, during which time they can use their notes, the library and other resources. They may even be permitted to use their fellow students and their tutors – though this can lead to problems. In a sense the one-week exam is simply an important end-of-course assignment with a one-week time limit though, if the time allowed for writing the exam is kept short, it is likely to be shorter in length than an assignment and so less of a burden for the markers.

Open book exam 18

A common criticism of conventional exams is that they test memory rather than any other ability. In practice professionals do not rely heavily on memory for information: they keep key textbooks and other reference sources at hand and consult them when they need to. They have to be familiar with these sources, but they probably do not need to memorise much of their contents. It does not seem sensible to deny students access to these everyday tools of the trade. Indeed the skills required to use them quickly and effectively may themselves be worth assessing.

In some subjects it goes without saying that students will have access to key reference sources; for example, astronomical tables for students of navigation. In other subject areas such as English literature it has become common for key texts to be available during the exam because students are being tested on what they can say about the texts, rather than what they can remember or quote from them. At the National Technical Highschool in Bergen, Norway, the engineering students have access to terminals linked to the main frame computer during their one-day final exams, and access to any computer programs they like, including programs or information they have previously entered themselves. So the solving of complex engineering problems in the exam more closely simulates the way working engineers operate. And allowing students access to such sources enables staff to set more complex questions than in conventional exams. There seems to be much more scope for open book exams than is usually recognised.

The main objections to open book exams come from tutors whose students are being tested on their memory for facts, definitions or algorithmic procedures, all of which are readily available in textbooks. In such cases the availability of books would largely invalidate the exam – but then one might question the value of such exams in the first place.

'Doing it' exam   19

Very often the real objectives of a course are not well matched by the kind of assessment used. In particular, courses with mainly practical aims are often assessed by end-of-course exams using standard essay questions (see item 1). To illustrate this point the example is given of an introductory module in history which ran in the first term of the first year of a three-year degree programme. It was designed to introduce alternative theoretical perspectives on social change so that in subsequent modules, which were mainly set in the context of particular periods and locations, students would be able to examine historians' evidence and explanations of evidence with an awareness of the theoretical perspectives of the writers.

The exam questions, however, were of the form:

Q.   Compare and contrast the theories of Condorcet and de Bonald.

Because they came from an A-level history background where they were expected to memorise material, students interpreted such questions as requiring them to memorise and list the main features of the theorists. Their exam answers revealed little about their ability to recognise theoretical assumptions in the writings of historians, and the nature of the exam did little to encourage the development of this skill during the course.

To turn this exam into a 'doing it' exam would require, for example, the selection of a recent history journal article, and the instruction to students:

Q.   Read this article and comment on the theoretical perspective of the author with particular reference to her interpretation of the evidence she presents.

This kind of task would test the objectives of the module and also orient students' efforts during the module towards those objectives rather than towards memorising.

A gap between theoretical underpinnings and practical objectives is often evident in education courses. Final exams commonly contain standard essay questions on the main theories of the psychology, sociology and philosophy of education. One course for further education tutors replaced such essay questions with a 'doing it' exam. One of the main aims of the course was that students should become more sophisticated in their ability to analyse practical teaching and identify ways of improving it. So, instead of being set a conventional exam, they were shown a videotape of a further education tutor teaching a class. They were then asked a series of practical questions about the tutor's performance which reflected psychological, sociological and philosophical issues. They were also asked to advise the tutor on teaching technique.

In law, 'doing it' exams can be based upon analysing cases or advising clients rather than simply upon recalling legal principles or precedents.

In science, 'doing it' exams can be based upon interpreting data or reading and commenting on a journal article describing experimental work, rather than upon recall of definitions, formulae or mathematical procedures.

'Doing it' exams can be extended over time if conventional two- or three-hour exam slots artificially constrain the nature of the 'doing' element (see item 17).

Restricted-choice exam   **20**

Most students revise selectively for their exams. Their estimate of how many topics to learn is based on the number of topics covered on the exam paper and the amount of choice they are given. So, for example, if the exam paper is of the standard type where students are asked to answer three questions out of eight, most will begin by cutting five topics out of their revision schedule. An exam pass on a course which is examined in this way is no guarantee of coverage of the course.

One way to ensure that students cover enough ground in their revision to satisfy you that they have engaged with the course is to adjust the number of questions and the extent of the choice in the exam.

Other ways include setting an obligatory broad-based question or an obligatory section containing short questions on a large number of topics.

You can of course take this further and eliminate choice entirely, in which case your exam paper will have the rubric 'Answer all the questions'.

A paper with no choice combines particularly well with a seen exam (see item 17). When students are first given the question paper, it can include, for example, the instruction 'These are the exam questions. The exam paper will contain three of them and you will be required to answer all three'. In this way students are obliged to study as many of the topics as you include on the list of questions.

Chapter 5
On-the-spot assessment

21 Viva

22 Exhibition

23 Observation

Viva   21

The viva, or oral exam, has a number of regular uses.

•   the assessment of oral fluency and comprehension, e.g. in language learning

•   the assessment of personal qualities and attitudes, or interpersonal skills

•   the assessment of the ability to think quickly and diagnose problems in novel situations, e.g. as a part of medical training

•   the further assessment of work previously submitted (e.g. a dissertation, a design, a recording of a musical performance) in order to check that the candidate is the author of the submitted work, to explore particular questions in more depth and to explore understanding further by raising new questions.

A viva can also be used for individuals or small groups of candidates who lack writing skills, who miss final written exams through illness, or whose marks fall on the borderline between two degree classifications.

The flexibility of vivas is their great asset. Issues can be picked up and explored in ways which are seldom possible in written tests with fixed questions which are the same for all students, and in which there is no opportunity to ask supplementary questions in cases of doubt. In even a short viva it is possible to gain a rich impression of the candidate.

The use of the viva presents some potential problems. It can be a very stressful experience for students. Examiners need to maintain a careful balance between the desire to keep the candidate relaxed and the need to ask challenging questions, and between the desire to keep the candidate talking and the need to direct the viva to particular areas. It can also be difficult to justify a decision afterwards in the absence of documentary evidence. Defence of viva decisions in the face of appeals tends to be based on the status and reputation of the examiner rather than on evidence.

Because of the potential problems, vivas are often used in conjunction with other assessment methods, for the purpose of increasing the range of information available about a candidate, rather than as a replacement for other assessment methods. This can be done in a variety of ways.

• a brief viva with a student after reading the student's essay, but before allocating a mark to it

• a brief viva about problems experienced during practical or project work, which are not mentioned in a written report, before allocating a mark to the report

• a viva as a preparation for other forms of assessment: to identify and diagnose weaknesses which require further attention from the student

• a viva during laboratory work, to assess students' understanding of what they are doing and encourage them to be thoughtful rather than simply to follow instructions.

Exhibition 22

It is usual for students on visual arts courses to mount exhibitions of their finished work in order to demonstrate its range and quality. An exhibition of this kind, which may or may not be supported by a student presentation, generally constitutes an important part of a student's assessment.

The exhibition can be used for assessment in a variety of other areas too. For example on one geography course students are required to produce a poster portraying one of the concepts of the course in a striking and informative way. The posters are exhibited for all to see and assessed without the support of verbal justifications by students.

Scientific and project work can also be exhibited, with photographs of equipment, clear graphs and diagrams, summaries and layouts to portray work undertaken. This encourages an emphasis on communication skills, especially graphic skills and the ability to write brief and clear summaries. It also tends to highlight the need to identify and demonstrate the purpose and conclusions of the project. Exhibitions 'sell' ideas and are used extensively in industry; this is a form of communication which students can benefit from encountering at first hand.

The preparation of exhibitions can be very engaging for students, and viewing them can be of great interest to others. So much of student learning is undertaken privately, even secretively, that an exhibition can have a powerful impact on students' motivation.

Observation   23

Observation is a common method of assessment in some subjects. For example, teacher training involves extended periods of classroom practice which are assessed by observation of the way the student handles the class. In Britain it is not possible to qualify as a teacher without passing this element of the assessment. Laboratory work too is often observed for assessment purposes, on the grounds that laboratory reports hide as much as they reveal. Practical training, from hairdressing to motor vehicle maintenance, generally involves observing and assessing the student in action. In these cases the use of observation is an explicit, formal part of the assessment system.

In many situations, however, observation is part of the process but only informally affects assessment. For example in studio-based work (e.g. art, design, architecture) the tutor will spend a lot of time observing the students working, but the assessment is, ostensibly, only of the end product: drawings, designs, plans or whatever. The final assessments are bound to be strongly influenced by the observations the tutor has made of the way these products were arrived at. It might be fairer in such circumstances to be explicit about the role of observation and about the criteria actually being used (for example, speed of working, ability to learn from mistakes, use of equipment). These criteria could be listed for students to see, to make them aware of what the observation consists of and encourage better practice (see Chapter 8).

In many areas where process is at least as important as product there is scope for using observation in a formal way:

- Observe and mark laboratory practice instead of marking laboratory reports.

- Observe and mark students' seminar performance instead of marking their seminar papers.

•   Observe students on field work (e.g. geology, surveying) instead of marking their reports and maps.

The main objection to using observation in assessment is that it is subjective and open to personal bias. Without a concrete product a student cannot appeal to a second marker (though in fact student teachers can appeal to an external examiner who then observes them teaching another class). There are several ways of minimising this problem.

•   Use observation checklists, rather than making a global judgement, so that marks are related to specific behaviours.

•   Use clear criteria with marks awarded for each criterion.

•   Use records such as audiotapes or videotapes which can be examined afterwards by a third party if necessary. They can also be used to give extra feedback to students.

Chapter 6

Assessment over time

Diaries and log books 24

A diary or log book is an individual record in which a student charts, day by day or week by week, her or his experience of a module or part of a module. It can be set as an alternative to or in addition to more traditional types of assessed writing.

The diary or log book is different from the essay or report in that it focuses on the process of learning rather than the outcome and also in that it tends to be informal in style and structure. It is a particularly appropriate method of assessment where the point of a module is the students' experience. This experience is not available from textbooks or lectures and has to be identified by the participants themselves.

Generally speaking, the difference between diary and log book is that the diary is a personal record whereas the log book is a more objective account of, for example, observations made, tasks completed and progress noted.

The rubric for the assessed diary could be, for example:

Keep a diary in which you write a brief summary of the activities of each week's session. Say what you have learned about yourself and others.

Or it could be less structured:

Keep a diary in which you write anything you like about your thoughts and feelings on the module.

It may be helpful, especially when students have not been assessed in this way before, if they are encouraged to read one another's diaries after a few weeks, so that they can see the potential of the diary form. Or they could read an extract from a published diary: for example the autobiography of

Eamon Dunphy, the Millwall footballer of the 1960s, illustrates what a reflective diary can look like.

A variation is that each week just one member of the class writes the diary episode, copies of which are then distributed to the rest of the students, so that they finish with a group record of the module. This can encourage group cohesiveness and trust, and it cuts down on the work for each individual. These diary episodes can be assessed and contribute to course marks.

The diary can also be used as a way into other more conventional academic forms of writing. Students who say they have a 'block' about writing essays or reports can be encouraged to sort out their ideas first in a diary where they are not under pressure to conform to a particular structure or style. Then, when they have got their ideas on paper, they should have the confidence to re-write them as an essay or report.

The log book can be used in conjunction with more formal types of assessed written work such as, for example, write-ups of science practicals, reports on industrial placements and work experience, and project reports of all kinds. If students have kept a record of their experience as it happened, they have the opportunity afterwards to reflect upon the progress they have made and the directions they have chosen.

The rubric for a science practical could be:

As you do this set of experiments, keep a log of everything you do and everything you observe, even if you can't see its relevance.

The rubric for students on sandwich placements could be:

At the end of each day, briefly note down what you did that day. Even if your experience seems disjointed at first, it will make more sense later if you have notes to look back on.

And for other kinds of project:

> Keep a log book of all the work you do for this project: books and articles read, action taken, decisions made, and also dead ends, apparently wasted effort etc. Your log should also contain a section specifying what you have learned from doing this project.

Criteria for assessing diaries and log books can be similar to those for other written work. Though there are no strict rules about structure or writing style, students can still be judged on such criteria as originality, commitment, skills of observation, analysis and synthesis, sensitivity, self knowledge etc. It is important to be explicit to students about criteria or to devise criteria together with students so that they understand them and are committed to them.

A set of criteria for assessing students' diaries on a midwifery degree is reproduced overleaf.

BSc Midwifery
Professional Skills II: Criteria for assessment

Write a diary of your experience of the module and evaluate your professional skills.

0 - 29   Does not constitute an answer to the question.

30 - 39   The student writes about professional skills but avoids any personal reflection or evaluation. Her language is full of cliches.

40 - 49   The student gives an account of the sessions on professional skills but lacks self knowledge and is dependent on ideas from books. Her language is impersonal.

50 - 59   The student gives an account of the sessions on professional skills and an account of herself in those sessions. She is honest and shows some self knowledge, supported by relevant examples. She is able to use personal language.

60 - 69   The student shows self knowledge and self awareness. She has insights about herself and the professional skills sessions and is able to evaluate both. Her illustrations are good. She is willing to take responsibility for herself and to learn. Her language is honest and personal.

70 +   The student shows the qualities of the above but in greater depth and with added flair and originality in her language.

Portfolios 25

Portfolios are commonly used in the selection and assessment of students of art, design, fashion etc. A student's portfolio will contain sketches, notes and versions of a final product as well as a number of finished pieces, selected from a year's work.

Portfolios can also be used in other subject areas where the assignments are not necessarily visual. Instead of handing in a small number of separate assignments, students produce a portfolio or file containing a larger number of shorter pieces for assessment.

A benefit of the portfolio method is that it encourages students to do lots of writing throughout a module and to be experimental in their writing, but without involving tutors in too much marking. It should also prompt those students who might otherwise be selective in their commitment to their studies to engage with the module as a whole.

Building up and presenting a portfolio of work involves students in collecting pieces of writing, evaluating them, and selecting the best - or those that go together to make the best portfolio. In other words, they are charting their own progress on the module, monitoring it and summarising it.

The portfolio method lends itself very well to student involvement in assessment. One model is described here.

Interim due dates are agreed on which students present their work to one another in small sub-groups of the lecture or seminar group and receive encouragement, criticism and suggestions for improvement. On the basis of this feedback they polish their work and select items for the portfolio, which is submitted on the final due date when it is assessed by the tutor. Whatever model is adopted, it is essential that students are clear about the criteria for assessment (see chapter 8) and that they know exactly what is expected of them (see below).

University of the West of England
Continental Literature: *Coursework portfolio*

4 - 8 pieces of work   **Interim due dates: first week in November**
                                            & last week of term 1
4,000 words   **Final due date: 11 February**

On this module you will be expected to do a number of pieces of written coursework in workshops, lectures and seminars. These pieces of writing could be, for example:

- the exploration of an idea / issue / theory presented on the module
- notes on a seminar discussion
- your response to one of the set texts
- a piece of imitative writing based on one of the set texts

You will be expected to present your writing to the group on the interim due dates so that you can receive feedback from your fellow students and tutors, with a view to polishing your work.

A selection of 4 - 8 pieces should be handed in as a portfolio on the final due date. The pieces may be of varying length but should total 4,000 words. They should also cover a range of aspects of the module and a range of types of writing and demonstrate some kind of coherence.

Criteria for assessment: see page 19 of the *Student Handbook*

Archives   26

On many courses, students do a series of separate assignments on separate modules and so are discouraged from making comparisons between their assignments. They are in fact almost certainly learning and developing from one assignment to another but they will probably remain unaware of their progress unless it is pointed out to them.

If you ask your students to start building up an archive of their assessed work and comparing their earlier efforts with their more recent achievements, this will reassure them about their progress and act as a motivator: students who have evidence of their progress are stimulated to achieve more.

You can get your students to keep an archive either by giving them encouragement in a general way or by using a more specific method, such as those described here.

Archives in the classroom
Ask your second-year students to bring in their first-year essays. Run a session in which they re-read the essays, specify what they have learned, and describe how they have progressed. They could do this in the round or in sub-groups, depending on numbers.

Ask the same question
If you set students an essay question in their first year and the same question again in their second or third year and ask them to compare the two, this will demonstrate to them how differently they write essays now. The best topics to use are those which lend themselves to treatment at various depths by students at different stages in their development. An example is the sociology essay question, 'What are some of the causes of juvenile crime?' This essay can be set at any stage from GCSE to MA or MSc. You can of course only use this method with the same group of students; if you want to use it on a modular course where students follow different routes, you

will need to set some of the key questions of the core modules in the foundation modules.

An incidental benefit of this method for the tutor is that the essays are likely to be easier and quicker to mark.

Show the same visual material
This method is similar to the previous one but covers a shorter time span.

Show students some visual material, for example a piece of anthropology film or a set of haematology slides. Show it to them at the beginning of a module or section of a course and ask them to note down what they see. Show it to them again when they have learned how to look at material from an anthropological or haematological perspective and get them to specify the progress that they have made.

This method can also be used with written materials, though student progress may be less tangible.

Use the same checklist
If you have an assessment checklist for your students, such as a set of objectives or criteria for marking, you can help them to monitor their progress by encouraging them to rate themselves regularly according to the checklist.

In a one-to-one teaching relationship with a student, as in the supervision of placements, projects etc., you can work together on the checklist. For example, Assessors of Supervised Practice who are responsible for assessing health visitor students on placement, work to a set of criteria devised by the English National Board. They meet their students regularly and go through the checklist together, identifying those criteria which the students have met and those where they need more training or experience: these are carried forward to the next meeting. The archive of checklists from earlier meetings gives the assessors the opportunity to point out to students how much progress they are making.

Chapter 7

Assessing projects and practicals

Assessing group project work   27

In group project work, students generally work as teams in small groups. Each group does a project and produces a report. One mark is then awarded to each group.

This type of assessment can give rise to problems, between groups and within groups.

Problems between groups relate to the level and range of marks. First, group work tends to be marked higher than individual work: groups can achieve more than individuals, and individual weaknesses tend to be covered up by the strengths of other group members. Second, group marks tend to vary less than individual marks: if groups are randomly formed, the average ability of the members of the groups will be similar and will lead to a narrow overall spread of marks. On many courses it is unacceptable for marks to be uniformly high (or, to put it technically, for the mean to be high and the standard deviation small).

Problems within groups relate to the differential contributions made by the group members. It is common for some students to contribute more than others to the work of the group and the production of the group report. Those who contribute less (either quantitatively or qualitatively) may deserve a lower mark than those who contribute more. Normally, however, group members are given the same grade because differences between group members' contributions are not apparent to the marker, who sees only the final report and not the process by which it came to be written. In this situation it is possible for low contributors to be 'carried' by the high contributors without incurring a penalty. The difficulty of arriving at a fair mark for individuals is one of the most common reasons for not using group work for assessment purposes, despite its many advantages for learning.

Some courses cope with these problems by weighting the mark for the group project in such a way that it counts for only a small proportion of the individual student's overall result. A more satisfactory solution is to try to build in mechanisms to allocate different marks to the different members of a group which reflect their relative contributions to the group's work.

Two methods are described here. The first method, shared group grade, is fairer to individuals and increases the spread of marks. The second, peer assessment of contribution to group, achieves both these aims and in addition lowers the average mark.

Shared group grade

While the tutor may not have much idea about individual students' contributions to a group project, the students themselves are in a very good position to make such judgments. Though the tutor can only award a mark to the group, the members of that group can be asked to distribute the mark between themselves in a way which they think reflects the relative contributions of individuals. For example if a group of five students were to be awarded 60% for a group report, they would be given $5 \times 60 = 300$ marks to distribute among themselves.

There are three ways in which groups tend to react in this situation. Some groups will agree at the start of the project that all marks will be shared equally at the end, in order to avoid unpleasantness. Such groups must face the risk of individual group members doing very little work.

Other groups will not discuss assessment at all until it is time to divide up the marks. They then find that they disagree about the basis upon which the marks should be allocated. Some will value creativity, some will value workload, some will value leadership, some will value the ability to communicate the project outcomes, and so on. Without prior agreement about criteria there are likely to be serious arguments.

Other groups again will decide at the start what criteria they will use in allocating marks, and will keep to these criteria. They will all be clear about what their contribution ought to be, and will be more likely to accept the final allocation of marks.

This third way of dealing with shared group grades is clearly the most satisfactory. You can help your students by organising discussion and negotiation of criteria at the start of the project. Or, alternatively, you can impose criteria of your own which the students then use to allocate the marks. It is crucial, however, that the criteria are made clear and accepted at the start of the project, and not hurriedly devised at the end.

There are two rather different ways in which criteria can be used:

• Students may naturally adopt different working roles within the group, or the project may even specify such roles. For example one student may become the chairperson, one the note-taker, one the data-analyser, one the report writer, one the 'ideas person' and so on. In this case assessment criteria can focus on how well each student performed her or his particular role.

• Every student may be expected to contribute equally to all aspects of the project (for example each writing one section of a group report). In this case each criterion should be applied equally to each student.

Peer assessment of contribution to group
Another solution to the problems associated with assessment of group project work - of unfairness to individuals, high average marks, and narrow bands of marks - is to weight individual students' marks according to their contribution to their group's work. Contributions are best judged by the group itself. In the rating sheet given as an example below, students are required to rate all other members of their group in terms of several key aspects of their contribution to the group's work. The criteria used here are for illustration only: other criteria concerning creativity, supportiveness in the group, or ability to keep to deadlines could equally be used. Alternatively, criteria could specify aspects of the project such as research, organisation of data, report writing, presentation of findings etc. The

average rating for each individual is then deducted from the group mark and allocated to that individual as her or his mark. In this case a student who made a major contribution to the group's work in every respect would have an average rating of 0 and receive the group grade. A student who contributed little to the group's work in all of these respects would receive the group grade minus 20 marks.

More or less severe penalties can be devised either by varying the number of criteria used, or by varying the penalties associated with criteria. The relative importance of criteria can be reflected in different penalties, as in the example. The criteria and size of penalties can be negotiated with the students, or even determined by them, at the start of the project so that they are aware of how they will be assessed, and have a commitment to the criteria.

Reference
For a detailed description of this method in practice, see Robert Conway, David Kember, Afara Sivan & May Wu, 'Peer Assessment of an Individual's Contribution to a Group Project' in *Assessment and Evaluation in Higher Education,* volume 18, no 1, 1993.

PEER ASSESSMENT OF CONTRIBUTION TO GROUP RATING SHEET

Student . . . . has contributed to the group's work in the following ways:

	Major Contribution	*Some Contribution*	*Little Contribution*
1. Leadership and direction	0	−1	−2
2. Organisation and management	0	−1	−2
3. Ideas and suggestions	0	−1	−2
4. Data collection	0	−2	−4
5. Data analysis	0	−2	−4
6. Report writing	0	−3	−6
Total penalty			

Supervisor's sheet   28

It is common for certain pieces of students' work to be assessed by two people rather than one in order to increase reliability and fairness. The larger and more important the piece of work (for example a final year project on a degree course) the more likely it is that a second marker will be involved.

Disagreements between markers arise for many reasons, some of which are unavoidable. But there is one important difference between the first and second marker which frequently leads to dissent and which can easily be remedied. The first marker is almost invariably the student's supervisor and will know the student and be aware of how she or he has tackled the project. The second marker is unlikely to know anything about this and will have to award marks without any contextual information. Some of this information is crucial to a fair assessment of the project. For example did the student receive a great deal of help in carrying out the work? Was the original idea for the work the student's own? Was a first draft submitted to and improved by the student's supervisor? While it is possible to mark a piece of work 'on its own merits' without regard for such information, assessment criteria usually include such factors as the initiative taken by the student, the creativity of the student and so on. Such criteria can only be implemented with the knowledge of the context in which the work was undertaken.

To give an example of the problems which can arise, a student could have left it until the last minute to start a project, then sought the advice of the supervisor for a suitable topic, been given help with references and experimental design, been given help with analysis and interpretation and been given detailed comments on a first draft of the report. The student might then submit quite a good final report. The first marker would know that little of this was the student's own work and give a moderate mark while a second marker would simply mark the report as seen and award a high mark.

To get around such problems you can simply provide the second marker with information about the way the work was carried out. One way of doing this is shown in the supervisor's sheet which follows. The information in this checklist is in the form of rating scales so as to provide information quickly and in a form which is easy to interpret. The supervisor completes this sheet and hands it to the second marker along with the student's work.

Supervisor's sheet

Name of Student ....

Supervisor ....

Second Marker ....

	suggested to student		received normal assistance		entirely student's own
1. Choice of topic	1	2	3	4	5
2. Theoretical contribution	1	2	3	4	5
3. Contribution to experimental design	1	2	3	4	5
4. Experimental technique	1	2	3	4	5
5. Data analysis and statistical treatment of results	1	2	3	4	5
6. Interpretation of results	1	2	3	4	5
	poor		normal		good
7. Impression of student's grasp of topic	1	2	3	4	5
	light		normal		heavy
8. Workload involved in the topic	1	2	3	4	5

Additional remarks from supervisor

....

....

Suggested mark .... *Signed* ....

Project exam   29

There are occasions where the main learning activity on a course is some kind of practical or project work but where there is still some necessity for a formal written examination. This may be because external validating bodies or professional bodies require an exam, or it may be because the staff consider an exam to be desirable.

Conventional exams, with their tendency to emphasise memorising and regurgitation of factual information, are quite unsuitable for a project-based course. This type of exam can completely distort the aims of the course by distracting students from their projects. However there are forms of exam which avoid these problems by asking students questions directly related to their project work.

On one estate management course, for example, students undertook a substantial case study involving the simulated purchase of a building site and its subsequent commercial development. This they wrote up in a report consisting of a log of their calculations, decisions, problems etc. (see item 24). The examination questions took the following form:

Q. If there was a three-month national building strike starting on week 3 of the simulation, how would this affect your handling of the case?

Q. If outline planning consent were granted for a competing major shopping precinct at the north end of the High Street on week 14 of the simulation (see details below), how would you advise your client?

Students would have their log books and other case material to hand (see item 18) and would be expected to use these in answering the questions. Such questions cannot be answered from memory, or even directly from this information, but only from students' experience and understanding of the case study.

In this first example, all students undertook the same project work individually. In the second example, below, students had been working in separate groups and individuals had been awarded a group grade. The exam in this case was designed to test individuals' understanding and to produce a mark for each individual student. The context was a catering management course in which groups of about 8 students tackled a simulated management problem. Within the groups students performed different roles (for example secretary, report writer) and so they almost certainly learned different things. The course was designed to apply management principles to a specific and complex situation. An exam was used to test individuals' ability to apply these principles to the work of their own groups.

Exam questions took the following form:

Q.   How can pricing and marketing policies influence other management decisions concerning catering outlets? Give specific examples from the simulation to illustrate your points.

The first part of this question is general, in that it is based on management principles learned at an earlier stage in the course. It is the second part which tests students' ability to apply these principles to their project work. This type of exam has the added advantage that if students know at the outset that they will be expected to answer questions of this form, they are more likely to be reflective about theory and general principles during the simulation than to get overwhelmed with practical details and forget the purpose of the exercise.

Instant lab report 30

Experienced scientists make full notes of their procedure, observations and results in the laboratory as they go along. Preliminary calculations are often made immediately in order to check that nothing is going seriously wrong. In contrast students are usually expected to produce neat lab reports for assessment at a later date. The effect this often has is to focus students' attention on producing good finished products, and to encourage leisurely post-hoc analysis and description of what happened, if not actual fiddling of results. Marks reflect students' abilities outside the laboratory rather than in it. Another effect is that students tend to work less quickly during practicals, noticing less about what is going on, and reflecting less about this. They follow instructions and adopt a narrow technical approach rather than a wider scientific approach to experimental work.

If instead, reports are required to be handed in at the end of the practical, this can have a dramatic effect on the way students undertake their work. They are likely to work faster, try to make more sense of what they are doing, make more observations and record these in better organised notes, and take more care when recording data. Obvious errors are more likely to be picked up, especially if calculations are undertaken immediately, and there may even be the opportunity to do the work again and correct it.

There is a risk that the quality of presentation may suffer if reports are written in the laboratory. Tutors can respond by acknowledging that reports will not look so good, and changing the criteria used in allocating marks, so that full recording of procedures and results will carry more weight than neatness. They can also give students uncompleted handouts on which to record procedures and results under headings and fill in spaces in response to questions. Initially it may be necessary to produce a handout specific to the experiment being undertaken, with standard details (e.g. materials and methods) typed in, and only a small number of sections for the students to complete but the amount of material on the handout can be reduced over time as students become more competent at writing their own instant reports.

Apart from clear benefits to student learning during practicals, this method frees students afterwards to do something more constructive than trying to remember what happened the previous week in order to write up a neat report. It also saves the tutor's time, as instant lab reports tend to be much shorter than those written afterwards.

Laboratory notes 31

Experienced scientists keep a notebook at hand during experimental work. They write down exactly what they do, what they notice, what goes wrong, what thoughts they have and so on. Notes are vital to the process of interpreting results and writing up an adequate account of the experiment. Some notes are so thorough that it is a only a short step from them to a full report.

Inexperienced students, in contrast, tend to take few and scrappy notes. Without material provided by the tutor they would find it impossible to remember the experiment and write a full account of it. Much 'fudging' of evidence and interpretation goes on afterwards because students simply do not have adequate notes from which to construct a full and honest report. This lack of notetaking may result from poor observation, or may even cause it: if observations have no apparent function then there is little point in making them. Students can end up doing experiments by simply following instructions in a mindless way.

If you want to encourage a more scientific and active approach to experimental work, and more observation and reflection during practicals, you can assess students' laboratory notebooks. This can be done as well as, or instead of, assessing laboratory reports which are written up afterwards.

Students may need guidance in taking laboratory notes. You could help them in the following ways.

• Recommend a particular type of notebook.

• Suggest headings and specific items.

• Show examples of useful laboratory notes.

- Have an exhibition of all students' notebooks half way through the year to guide future notetaking (see item 22).

- Pass students' notebooks round the class for comment and comparison.

- Clarify your criteria for assessing such notes, e.g.
  fullness   range of observations
  clarity   neatness
  adequacy of diagrams   specification of units
  etc.

It is important, in assessing notebooks, that you do not pervert their purpose. If students start handing in second drafts, neat versions, and notes which were obviously written largely after the experimental work, in order to get better marks, then you may have to take other action to retrieve the situation (e.g. see item 30).

Laboratory notebooks may also be used to record subsequent thoughts derived from further reading, analysis of data, seminars and so on. The notebook then becomes a record of the development of students' understanding of the subject, and can be used as the basis for reflection. You could suggest that two pages headed 'thoughts' or 'discussion' be left blank between experiments, to be completed at a later stage as ideas arise.

It is common for such laboratory notebooks to be handed in only at the end of the year. However, the process of writing such a notebook can encourage so much reflection, self assessment and learning that it can be valuable to make them more central to the learning process by assessing them more frequently and organising seminars, tutorials or more informal discussions around them.

Chapter 8

Criteria

Specifying criteria   **32**

One of the most effective ways of getting students to write assignments in the way you want them to, and to improve the quality of their assignments, is simply to tell them what your assessment criteria are. If students know how marks are gained and lost this will have a powerful effect on their behaviour.

Even when guidelines for writing assignments are provided, students do not always recognise that they also contain implicit, or even explicit, marking criteria. For example one set of guidelines, 'Notes on the presentation of experimental reports' for psychology students, contains predictable sections on layout, headings and so on, but also advice such as:

> Individual style and opinion are of little interest compared with a clear and lucid description . . . . Personal opinions should be avoided as far as possible and where mentioned should be identified as such. Use of the first person singular should be avoided.

Criteria such as these are not only related to marking; they define the whole nature of the learning task which students are confronted with. It is vital that students recognise them if they are to go about their studying in an appropriate way.

Sometimes criteria are specific to a particular subject, or to the way that subject happens to be taught in a particular institution - and are quite unpredictable by an outsider. For example, one set of 'Guidelines on essay writing' for geography students illustrates such local criteria:

> (ii) subheadings are necessary. These should not necessarily be one-word telepathic subheads – they should express concisely what is to be found in the section following them. (Do not get the wrong idea about subheads. They do *not* 'break up' an essay – on the contrary,

they make it flow and integrate the elements of argument in the reader's mind. They make for vastly greater clarity: most published academic work uses them, so do most newspapers – in both, communication is important. *Use subheads!*)

In a different department just along the corridor from these geographers, students are marked down when they use subheadings, let alone the kind of punctuation used here. It is clearly important to let the students know exactly what the local criteria are.

These criteria can be made more specific if the guidelines are presented *in terms of* the criteria, as in the following example taken from a handbook for humanities students at the University of the West of England.

In awarding a grade to work, humanities staff will be assessing the extent to which it displays, <u>in varying strengths and combinations,</u> the following characteristics. These apply particularly to essays and examination essay answers, but also to dissertations and practical/project reports. Other characteristics are taken into account when awarding grades to, say, journals or field study notebooks.

UNDERSTANDING   This refers to the extent to which the basic issues and arguments relating to a topic have been grasped and placed in the more general context of the module or academic discipline. Severe weakness at this level can produce a 'fail' grade.

COVERAGE   Essay/examination questions are designed to specify the material required. Thorough coverage is necessary to gain a Lower Second Class or above. General statements should be supported by data or examples.

ORGANISATION   Written work should be organised in a logical and clearly-argued manner in relation to the specific title or question. Work which merely

	throws points together is unlikely to gain more than a Third Class.
RESEARCH	Evidence of wide reading is an important criterion, and work based on a restricted range is unlikely to gain more than a Lower Second Class. Tutors can advise on an appropriate range for particular topics but this is also a matter for individual exploration. It is also important for students to use a system of referencing and a bibliography so that it is quite clear which sources are used in coursework essays, dissertations and reports.
COMMUNICATION SKILLS	Good English expression is important for stating arguments clearly. Weaknesses here (including spelling) may lead to a reduction in grade, and advice about any problems should be sought at an early stage of the course.
ORIGINALITY	This is more difficult to define, but it may involve some unique insight, or a strikingly different and lucid argumentative organisation of the material; when combined with other characteristics it may result in a First Class grade.

The criteria in the three examples above are general in the sense that they apply to all reports, or all essays, in a subject area. However it is often the case that criteria vary considerably from one assessed task to another, and even from one tutor to another, even within a subject area, in a way which reflects a range of different educational goals. For example scientific laboratory work can be undertaken for many different reasons:

－ to develop skills with equipment

- to demonstrate phenomena
- to develop general scientific methodology
- to aid the grasp of new concepts
- to improve report writing
- to increase accuracy in measurement
- to practise mathematical methods

and so on. These different aims are likely to be reflected in marking criteria, if not in the kind of reports students are required to write. It is crucial that students are told what they should be concentrating on. A laboratory briefing could take the following form:

> The experiment today involves sensitive and tricky equipment which is new to you, and difficult measurements. Even small errors in your measurements will invalidate the experiment. So you should concentrate on accuracy, and on calculating the degree of error involved in your measurements and calculations. I'm not interested, today, in a long theoretical introduction to your reports, or an extended discussion of your results. Concentrate on measurement issues and error. You will be marked largely on how accurate your results are.

Assignment criteria can be made more specific if they are presented in terms of degree classifications, as in the following example: a set of criteria for writing a book review.

Write a review of a book of your choice for your professional journal.

0-29%   Does not constitute an answer to the question.

30-39% Lacks many of the characteristics of a book review. Gives inadequate information about the book being reviewed.

40-49% Has basic characteristics of a book review. Gives basic information about the book being reviewed.

50-59% Has characteristics of a book review. Gives information about the book being reviewed. Has inadequate evaluation.

60-69% Reads like a book review. Gives full and relevant information about the book being reviewed. Evaluates the book being reviewed and judges its suitability for the readership of the journal.

70+%   Suitable for publication in the journal: is informative, evaluative, creative and interesting to read.

Staff marking exercise 33

If you were to ask the members of a course team what their criteria for assessment were, it is likely that the answers would be so general and all-embracing as to be unhelpful. Such generalisations can also mask real differences in tutors' values and perceptions of the aims of a course. One way of highlighting these is to run a staff marking exercise. In such an exercise, tutors get together with copies of student assignments on the same topic, mark them, and compare their marks and comments. This then leads to a general discussion about assessment. The purpose of the exercise is not to mark the students, but to provide a forum in which tutors can discover how they compare with one another. In particular it can clarify the criteria that are being used in assessment.

In the Open University, where many people teach on the same course, it is common at the start of the year to get all the tutors together and give them some samples of student work to mark. The ensuing discussions help to clarify the aims of the course, and also encourage consistency between markers. Tutors can see very quickly whether they are adopting different standards and marking more strictly or more generously than their colleagues.

Even when a set of criteria for student assignments exists (see item 32), this may not lead to consistency between markers if there are value differences. For example, tutors often put a different value on the dutiful, painstaking but dull piece of work and the quirky, unstructured witty piece. It is easy to include these elements in a list of criteria, but harder to be explicit about their relative importance. Staff marking exercises give an opportunity to explore these issues.

The following points are offered as guidance for running a marking exercise:

a   Choose real examples of student work as a basis for discussion. Abstract discussions are much less fruitful. Even one example is very much better than none. Three or four examples are usually plenty: more can cause confusion and introduce more complexity and variation than staff can handle.

b   Choose examples of moderate quality or perhaps of uneven quality with both good and bad features. It is relatively easy to agree on what is outstanding or awful, and little is learned through such easy agreements.

c   Get staff to mark the examples all at the same time, during the exercise. If they do the marking too far in advance there is a danger that they will either have forgotten details or formed a fixed and limited impression, perhaps with the expectation of having to defend it in public.

d   Do not at first expect staff to make public their marks or views of the examples. Allow them the opportunity to compare these with one or two others 'in private' first. This will make it much more likely that they will be flexible and receptive to the reality of differing values and perceptions which will inevitably be revealed.

e   An attempt should be made to extract and discuss broad differences of principle underlying the differences in marks even if this proves difficult, rather than to go straight into seeking compromise and consensus on marks. There is unlikely to be any long term effect on consistency unless the broad issues are tackled.

f   Outcomes of the exercise should be clearly recorded to prevent staff sliding back into their old patterns.

g   Students should be informed of issues which have been resolved concerning criteria and standards.

Marking schemes 34

Marking schemes consist of information on how marks are allocated to answers. They perform two main functions: one for the student and one for the marker.

They help the student to see, on a question paper, how marks are to be distributed between questions. For example it is common in science subjects for the first section of an exam to contain factual and short answer questions and for the second section to contain more open-ended problems requiring more understanding. Typically the questions in the first section each attract fewer marks than those in the second section, and even if there are more questions in the first section, and it takes up more space on the paper, fewer marks in total are allocated to the section. It is important for students to recognise this if they are to distribute their time and effort sensibly between questions. In fact understanding the balance of such marking schemes is crucial to learning strategies during the course and to revision techniques before exams.

Marking schemes can be used even more specifically to orient students' effort in desired directions. For example with structured questions containing several elements (see item 3) it is helpful to students to specify the marks which will be allocated to each element.

Marking schemes also perform useful functions for the marker. Where many different markers are involved in assessing answers to the same questions it is common practice to use marking schemes which refer explicitly to the content of answers. A common type of marking scheme specifies particular items which should for example be mentioned by students, briefly discussed, or presented in diagrams. Students accumulate marks according to how many of these specified 'targets' they manage to hit. The purpose of such marking schemes is to increase the consistency with which different markers award marks to the same answer.

The following example illustrates the two main purposes of marking schemes. First, the exam paper:

B/TEC Higher Certificate in Applied Biology Year 1
MICROBIOLOGY THEORY

Instructions: Answer BOTH questions in Section A (40%) and any THREE in Section B (60%)

Section A (40%)
1   In an experiment to determine the rate . . . .
    [a description of an experiment, and some experimental data, followed]

Answer each of the following:
a   Plot the data on a single side of graph paper and in the most appropriate manner. (12 marks)

b   Calculate the mean generation time of the bacterium in the two media. (2 marks)

c   Explain why the innoculum was washed and predict the likely result of the experiment if the innoculum had been taken directly from a nutrient broth culture. (4 marks)

d   In this experiment, colony counts were used to determine the increase in population size during the incubation. Suggest another method which could have been used to measure the increase. (2 marks)

Without this guidance on the way marks were to be allocated it seems unlikely that students would have guessed that the calculation in section (b) and the suggestion in section (d) were only worth a sixth of the marks of the graph in section (a). This guidance should result in students spending more than half the time allocated for this question on the graph. A tutor's marking scheme was written for this exam paper. The scheme for question 1 is reproduced below. The number of marks which can be awarded for each element of the answer is specified, as is the maximum number of marks for each section.

ANSWERS

1 a Graph: (12 marks)
   Title: **Growth** (0.5) of a **bacterium** (0.5) in **two media** (0.5) at **30°C** (0.5) with **aeration** (0.5).

   X-axis: **time** (0.5); **hours** (0.5); **sensible scale** (0.5).

   Y-axis: **counts** (0.5); **volume** (0.5); **log plot** (0.5); **sensible scale** (0.5).

   Plots: **correct plot** of each set of data (2.0); **sensible line** for growth pattern for each set of data (2.0); **zero time count** calculated (2.0).

   b (2 marks) **2 values** within 10% (2.0).

   c (4 marks) To **remove** nutrient broth from innoculum (2.0). **No lag phase** in nutrient broth (1.0). **Growth rates** of cells in defined medium would be **different** (1.0). **Any other** sensible suggestions (1.0).

   d (4 marks) **Absorption** (2.0). **Any other** reasonable suggestion (2.0).

   20 marks total

This kind of marking scheme is likely to increase consistency between markers. It can also cause unfairness if students offer valid comments, or go about answering questions, in ways which are not mentioned in the scheme; terms such as 'Any other sensible suggestions' are an attempt to provide for such variation.

Hidden criteria   **35**

Hidden criteria are those assessment criteria which affect students' grades but which are not made explicit. For example many tutors dislike errors in spelling and punctuation. Tutors often have strong views about length, legibility, colloquial language, badly labelled diagrams, failure to state units of measurement and so on. They may admit to their colleagues that such factors influence their response to their students' work, but they may not correct them or even comment on them to the students themselves. Even if they do give their students feedback on these issues, the students may not realise the effect they have on marks.

Studies of assessment systems suggest that hidden criteria are widespread, and that they are sometimes quite different from, or even contradictory to, the stated criteria. For example there may be fine-sounding public statements about the importance of creativity and a student's individual contribution to a piece of work, whereas in reality marks may be awarded for following detailed procedures to a prespecified pattern.

Students expect tutors to differ, and many actively look out for clues as to what particular marking foibles each has. If you want to take the guessing out of this process and you want your students to know what your own hidden criteria are, this is what you should do:

a   Write down all those features of student work which influence your perception, either positively or negatively.

b   Hand this list to your students and ask them if they have any suggestions to add.

Project criteria   36

The arguments for having clear assessment criteria for project work are much the same as those for having criteria for any other kind of work (see item 32) but projects pose additional problems. In essay writing it is the product which is assessed and, while the skills and processes by which the product was produced may be assessed indirectly, these are not open to scrutiny. In project work the process is often the most important element, and the skills involved in undertaking the project and presenting its outcomes are generally more important than the outcomes themselves. Since the choice of criteria dictates the direction and form of project work, criteria for marking projects should clearly reflect these different educational goals and direct students' attention towards these goals.

A second difficulty with project criteria is that projects tend to be open-ended: outcomes are inherently unpredictable. This means that criteria need to be couched in somewhat general terms. Criteria which specify content on the one hand or criteria which specify form or process on the other hand will tend to result in a narrowing of the scope of the project. For short projects, for inexperienced students, and when educational goals for the project are tightly specified in terms of content, this may be desirable. For open-ended projects designed to give students scope for exploration and creativity such criteria would be counterproductive.

The concern for process and for open-endedness is illustrated in the following extract from a list of criteria used by more than 50 mathematics tutors at the University of Southampton:

> Supervisors are reminded that their assessment of the way in which the student has worked during the course is to be taken into account together with the assessment of the project reports. This should be reflected in the written comments, and may be relevant to the criteria under headings B and C below.

A	Exposition	Mathematical accuracy
		Clarity
		Literary presentation
B	Literature	Understanding
		Relating different sources
		Finding new sources
C	Originality	Examples cited
		Examples constructed
		New treatments and proofs of standard results
		Simple generalisations
		Original researches
D	Scope of topic	Conceptual difficulty
		Technical difficulty
		Relationship with previous studies
		Relevance of material included
		Coverage of the topic

The example which follows, from the School of Engineering at the University of Bath, includes not just a detailed set of criteria, but a grading scheme for each criterion, and a system of allocating marks under each of the main headings. It can serve as a profile at the same time as being used as a marking scheme (see items 37 and 34). Many of the criteria here are concerned exclusively with process and skills and could not be applied in a situation where assessment is based on the final report alone. For example, in section 1.6 the student's log book is assessed (see also item 24). These criteria, focusing as they do on process, entail close supervision by the tutor throughout the project.

These criteria also reflect a further interesting characteristic of projects: the extended period of time usually associated with project work allows proper revision and redrafting of final reports. Here the draft report is allocated more marks than the final report, and criteria for the final report include the response of the student to criticism of the draft. Criteria for the draft are concerned with substantive issues, while those for the final report focus more on presentation and style.

Project marking form

MARKS ALLOCATION

Carrying out	(50%)		%
Log Book	(5%)		%
Draft Report	(30%)		%
Final Report	(15%)		%

%

Supervisors should enter their grading of the student's performance under these headings: they should indicate where they are inapplicable, and add any special aspects in section 4. The items are not weighted, so there is no requirement to convert the gradings into marks.

O = outstanding   E = excellent G = good S =satisfactory   P = poor I = inadequate

	O	E	G	S	P	I	COMMENTS
1. CARRYING OUT 1.1 Approach Exploration and enquiry Literature and background search Setting objectives Preparation of programme							
1.2 Implementation Decisions on test facilities and instrumentation Design of rigs and apparatus Building and commissioning rigs Setting up calibration							

	O	E	G	S	P	I	COMMENTS
1.3 Experiments Logical planning Accuracy and relevance of measurements Overcoming difficulties Modifications during progress							
1.4 Computing Modelling Programming Analysis Presentation							
1.5 Evaluation Study of previous theories Prediction based on theory Analysis of experimental results Relation between theory and results							
1.6 Log Book Maintained as instructed Standard of entries							

O = outstanding   E = excellent   G = good   S = satisfactory   P = poor   I = inadequate

	O	E	G	S	P	I	COMMENTS
O = outstanding E = excellent G = good S = satisfactory P = poor I = inadequate							
2. MANUSCRIPT DRAFT REPORT Structure of the report Clarity of argument Balance of sections Validity of results Justification of conclusions Details; figures; titles; references Achievement of objectives							
3. FINAL REPORT Response to criticisms of draft Layout of report Standard of execution Style							
4. SPECIAL ASPECTS							

5. SUPERVISOR'S COMMENTS ON STUDENT'S PERFORMANCE AND ATTITUDES
e.g. response to advice and criticism, initiative, determination to succeed, dependence on instruction, powers of innovation, enthusiasm, perseverance

Profiles 37

The outcome of most assessment systems is a single grade or mark which is supposed to indicate the student's overall ability or achievement. This grade or mark may have been arrived at through the assessment of many distinct areas of knowledge and skills, and the student is likely to have achieved more in some areas than others. None of these different achievements, or weaknesses, are reflected in the final mark in a way which can be interpreted by an outsider (or even, in many cases, by students or their tutors). Profiling has the opposite goal. The aim of profiling is not to summarise all the component elements in a single mark but to represent the component elements separately. Its purpose is primarily informative: to provide the student, the tutor, and outsiders, with information which can guide further learning, teaching and selection.

By specifying the key elements on which assessment is based, profiling also identifies criteria. Very often this is done by specifying objectives, i.e. statements of what the student should be able to *do* at the end of the course. The final profile can be seen as a statement of which objectives have been achieved and also, perhaps, to what standard.

The example which follows is a profile statement taken from a B/TEC Mathematics I unit which is part of a course in technician studies. The breakdown of general objectives makes it clear what is to be learned. The performance indicator is designed to show the extent to which the objectives have been achieved. This form can be updated as the student is assessed. A full profile of the student's learning is available at each stage in the course, indicating where further effort is called for, and where assessment is required. At the end of the course the profile indicates what the student can do, and can not do, and any gaps will indicate areas where the student's ability has not been established.

The use of profiles has become widespread in the assessment of personal qualities, partly out of a desire to provide clear criteria and reduce variability between different assessors, but also to provide feedback for students and information for future employers. As with all uses of criteria, the nature of the profile should be made clear to students at the start of the course, and assessments should be made and discussed at several points during the course, and not just at the end.

Reference
J. Mortimore, *Profiles in Action,* Further Education Unit, 1984.

TECHNICIAN EDUCATION COUNCIL
Profile Statement for a Course in Technician Studies

Unit: Mathematics 1 (U80/683)
Student:
College:
Date:

	Performance			
Unit General Objectives for the student are that he/she:	NA	3	2	1
A. Arithmetic operations				
1. Evaluates expressions involving integer indices and uses standard form				
2. Evaluates expressions involving negative and fractional indices and relates indices and logarithms				
3. Ensures that answers to numerical problems are reasonable				
4. Understands and uses tables and charts				
5. Performs basic arithmetic operations on a calculator				
B. Algebra				
6. Uses basic notation and rules of algebra				
7. Multiplies and factorises algebraic expressions involving brackets				
8. Solves, algebraically, simple equations and linear simultaneous equations				
9. Evaluates and transforms formulae etc.				

NA   means not assessed
3   means the student has been assessed but needs more practice
2   means the student has shown basic competence
1   means the student has shown a high degree of competence

General Comments:

Signed: Status:

Criterion-referenced assessment 38

Much of the assessment which takes place in education is norm-referenced. This means that the assessment indicates how good one person is in relation to the total group being assessed. A graduate with a first class honours degree in biology, for example, is among the top 5-10% of graduates. And a student with a grade A in A-level history is among the best group of students who took that A-level exam that year. What such assessment systems cannot tell you is what these students know or can do. A biology graduate from one university will know quite different things from a biology graduate from another university, even though they will be of roughly equivalent ability in some general sense. Similarly, in the case of students with A-level history, it is not possible to tell what they can actually do, or which particular aspects of history they would be able to explain. Norm-referenced assessment is often used when tough selection decisions have to be made. For example it is common for science laboratory facilities to be insufficient to cope with all first year students continuing into the second and third year of a course. If only 75% of the first year students can be accommodated then 25% have to be failed in their first year exams *regardless of how competent they are.*

In contrast, criterion-referenced assessment measures how an individual has performed, quite independently of how others have performed. A clear example of a criterion-referenced test is the high jump. There is an absolute dividing line between 'passing' or 'failing' a 2-metre high jump, the criteria for which are easy to specify and apply, and which have nothing to do with the performance of others.

There are a number of subject areas in education where criterion-referenced assessment would make a lot more sense than the present norm-referenced assessment. Instead of being able to say about a course: 'Those who have passed this course are among the best 80% of their group' it would then be possible to say: 'Those who have passed this course can all do the following things: . . . .'

One such subject area is construction engineering. It is often argued that the reason for the engineering syllabus commonly being so full, and for teaching methods being so tutor-dominated, is that there is a certain body of knowledge which all engineers must know 'or their bridges will fall down'. However in practice the assessment system used is invariably norm-referenced. That is, all it indicates is how good students are in relation to one another. Engineering students with a pass degree will be among the bottom 20% or so of their year. They may also have got half of every question they answered in the final exam wrong. It is possible to gain recognition as a member of a professional engineering society without being able to do anything at all 100% correctly, simply by avoiding being in the bottom group.

This situation would not be tolerated for driving tests. It would clearly not be acceptable if candidates could pass their driving test while staying on the road for only half of the time, or while being able to change gear correctly but not being able to steer. For such assessments there needs to be a set of criteria *all* of which must be met by candidates if they are to pass. And there is little sense in producing a mark in such a test. Either candidates are good enough to be allowed out on the roads on their own or they are not. The driving test is a criterion-referenced test: whether candidates pass or fail does not depend on how good they are compared with others taking the test at that time, but only on whether they can meet a range of performance criteria.

Such assessment schemes have clear advantages. Students know what constitutes an acceptable learning outcome and they can easily tell when further study is or is not necessary. For employers or others who want information about the abilities of students a criterion-referenced system of assessment is of particular value because it enables reasonable predictions about what the student will be able to do.

The implementation of criterion-referenced assessment is often associated with the use of objectives and profiles (see item 37).

Chapter 9

Feedback to students

SAQs 39

The acronym SAQ first became widely known through its use by the Open University in their printed learning materials. It stands for Self Assessment Question. In Open University course materials you will find SAQs used extensively, interspersed through the text and collected together in clusters at the end of sections and booklets. Their purpose is primarily to provide a device through which students can engage in an active thoughtful way with the material instead of simply reading it passively. SAQs may require the student to give a written response, check through a previous section, interpret a set of data, read sections from other books, or simply give the topic some quiet thought before progressing to the next section. Answers are given to provide feedback, sometimes immediately after the question, but more usually at the end of the booklet. The answers allow students to check whether they are on the right track, and may include remedial advice or refer the student to the section of the booklet or other books where the basis for the answer can be found. The answers come in a variety of forms such as checklists, model answers, discussions and so on.

There is no live involvement of the tutor in this questioning and answering. SAQs are designed for students to use on their own - and they do this in a bewildering variety of ways, including looking up the answer and then trying to work out the relationship between it and the question. Although designed for use in distance-learning material, the idea of offering ques- tions *and answers* for students to use in their private study can equally well be used in other areas of education. To some extent the kinds of problem sheets commonly used in science and technology are like SAQs except that answers are usually given out at a later date rather than being available to students along with the questions to use as they see fit.

There are many possible applications of SAQs. Some examples follow:

•	lecture handouts with SAQs to encourage subsequent thought about the lecture

• reading lists with SAQs for each topic or book to give feedback on private reading

• SAQs displayed on an overhead projector transparency at the start of a lecture, as students settle down, with the answers provided on a second transparency before the lecture starts

• sets of SAQs on special handouts for each section of a course

• SAQs for each section of a course reader or set text.

By offering SAQs you will be identifying for students what you consider to be important issues on the course, and your answers will enable them to judge whether they are giving enough attention to these issues.

Student requests for feedback   **40**

Writing comments on students' work is a time-consuming part of a tutor's job and can be very discouraging: often there seems to be little evidence that students have taken the feedback seriously or even, at times, understood it.

One way of ensuring that students pay more attention to your feedback, and that it will be seen to answer their needs directly, is to ask them what kind of feedback they want. If it is what they have asked for, they will be motivated to take it seriously. They are in the best position to know what their difficulties are and to judge what kind of feedback is helpful.

Students' requests for feedback can be elicited from individuals or from the group as a whole.

If you want requests from individual students, you can ask them when they do a piece of assessed writing to add a note at the end specifying what kind of feedback they would like. (You can include this in a handout of your assignment titles.) Your students will probably need some encouragement the first time and an explanation of why you think it is a good idea and maybe some examples of the kind of requests they might make.

When invited to choose, some students just ask for general comments but given the opportunity most students find it easy to identify areas where they have difficulty, and ask specific questions such as 'I'm not sure if I have answered the question. Have I?' Often they write at some length.

Here are some examples of requests for feedback from students on a literature course:

> nb Sue – could you give this the full treatment, pointing out spelling mistakes, grammatical errors etc. And Sue, just one thing – be kind.

Dear Sue

Please ignore my spelling and typing errors as i think they are totaly irrelivant to the arguements I am trying to put across. Apart from this please feel free, and I would like to invite you to criticise my work on every point that you think is relivant. The more criticism I get on the essay the more I can put right in the next.

Sue, could you let me know your opinion on my style, as well as the actual content. Don't worry about spelling unless it's really awful!

I think I have expressed myself clumsily in this analysis – especially in terms of the way my sentences are organised or disorganised. The kind of feedback I would like is (a) to see whether you think it is disjointed, and (b) for you to show me how you go about doing this type of exercise.

These students clearly wanted rather different kinds of feedback, and what suited one would have annoyed another.

If you want a request from the whole group, you can set up a pyramid exercise to enable students to clarify and pool their ideas. Pyramid exercises operate in four stages: first, students work on their own, then in pairs, then in fours, and finally as a total group. You could say:

Stage 1

'I'd like you to spend five minutes looking through the comments on your marked essays from the course so far.'

Stage 2

'Now, in pairs, give each other examples of good feedback and bad feeedback. Take five minutes to talk about this.'

Stage 3

'Now get into fours and draw up a list of guidelines for feedback which I can use as a checklist when I am marking your work. Use examples from your marked work, or use your own ideas, or both. One member of the group act as scribe and write down the list. You've got fifteen minutes for this.'

Stage 4

'Now I'd like the scribe from each group in turn to read out that group's list and I'll make a total list on the blackboard. When we've got the whole list written up, we'll see if any points are duplicated or if there are any which present problems. What we are working towards is a list which you and I can all agree to. O.K., can we start with the scribe from this group?'

(See also item 41)

If students are asked what kind of feedback they want, not only are they more likely to receive it but in specifying it they are getting practice at self assessment. It is also better for their self respect if they identify their strengths and weaknesses themselves. An additional benefit is that their requests often constitute feedback to the tutor or her or his usual methods. For example, a student may say: 'Please try to give me constructive criticism and not just praise' or 'Please try to find a kinder way of telling me when I misunderstand things'.

Feedback checklists   41

A feedback checklist is a set of guidelines for giving feedback to students. Tutors can use a feedback checklist to evaluate the quality of their own written comments on students' work.

Such a checklist can be devised and administered by the head of department or course tutor. The Open University, for example, operates a checklist system whereby staff tutors (who supervise the tutors who mark students' work) evaluate a sample of each tutor's marking against a checklist which includes such items as the balance between single word and full sentence comments, and the balance between positive and negative comments.

The checklist does not have to be imposed from above, however. Members of a course team can devise and administer their own. The items in such a list could arise out of discussions following a staff marking exercise (see item 33).

Alternatively, individual tutors can make their own lists, in consultation with their students. Overleaf is a checklist which was drawn up by a group of Further Education Teaching Certificate students at the then Bristol Polytechnic, using the kind of pyramid discussion exercise described in item 40.

GUIDELINES FOR GIVING FEEDBACK

1. Keep the time short between the student writing and the feedback

2. Where possible give instantaneous feedback

3. Tie in the grade with the comment (i.e. not 'An excellent piece of work: D')

4. Summarise the comments and flag the fact that it's a summary

5. Balance positive with negative

6. Flag what is positive and what is negative

7. Negative points should be constructive

8. Indicate how the student can improve

9. Follow up with oral feedback

10. Aim for a dialogue

11. Encourage students to evaluate themselves

12. Encourage students to ask for feedback elsewhere (e.g. from other students or other members of staff)

13. Ask students what kind of feedback they want

14. Make the criteria clear when setting the work and relate the feedback to the criteria

15. Distinguish between different skills (e.g. the student may have lots of good ideas but be poor at spelling)

16. Offer help (e.g.'Would you like a refresher course on the use of the apostrophe?')

17. Give affective feedback (e.g. 'It's really frustrating reading your essay because it could have been good but . . .' or 'I enjoyed reading this . . .')

18. Make further suggestions (e.g. for further reading or developing ideas)

19. Distinguish between formative and summative assessments

20. Give periodic oral feedback on rough drafts

Assignment attachment forms   **42**

Traditionally, higher education staff have marked students' assignments with great care, correcting errors of expression in the text, writing detailed comments in the margins and providing a substantial amount of individualised feedback in summary. In many institutions, as class sizes increase, marking of this quality is now proving impossible to sustain and some tutors are reducing their marking load and standardising aspects of their marking practice by using assignment attachment forms.

The assignment attachment form is written to a *pro forma*, which is either printed and filled in by hand or stored on a computer disk and keyed in on the word processor. It replaces all other types of written feedback. (This is important: if tutors allow themselves to write comments on students' scripts as well as filling in the form, they gain nothing.)

It is common for tutors to be reluctant to move from traditional methods to something more streamlined. They feel it is a dereliction of duty not to correct, for example, every error in spelling and punctuation which students make, forgetting how many students in fact ignore that type of feedback. It is possible with the assignment attachment form to identify students who need help with spelling and punctuation and offer it to them, safe in the knowledge that only those students who are keen to benefit will come forward.

Four examples of assignment attachment forms are shown on the following pages. Their particular benefits are described here.

Positive and negative (Twentieth Century Continental Literature)
This is an open form with a lot of scope for individualised feedback. Specifying positive and negative aspects makes it easier for the marker to focus the feedback. Students have said they prefer this format to the traditional method because they are guaranteed some positive feedback and, more importantly, they feel that in the 'Suggestions for improvement'

section they have something to carry forward to their next assignment.

Constants and variables (Laboratory report marking sheet)
This form is organised according to the sections of the assignment. These remain constant for every assignment of this type though the guidelines and the weighting of marks can vary. The tutor fills in the 'guidelines' and 'maximum marks' columns before each practical and gives copies of the form to the students. This makes it clear to them how marks will be awarded for that particular piece of work. The students return their forms with their completed reports and the tutor then allocates marks and gives feedback by writing comments under the different headings.

Criteria (Co-counselling assignment)
This form is organised according to the criteria specified for the particular assignment. This makes it easy to fill in, as well as ensuring that the marking relates directly to the criteria. Forms with explicit criteria also increase the likelihood that different markers will arrive at similar marks.

Checklist (DASS Psychology Programme)
Here criteria are presented as a checklist with a five-point marking scale. Of the four, this is the form which is the quickest to use but it is also the most impersonal.

Twentieth Century Continental Literature
Second assignment

Note: If you would like a tutorial on this assignment please sign your name on the list which is on the door of my office (3 CK29).

From Sue Habeshaw

To Student no ...

Some things I like about your assignment:
....
....
....

Suggestions for improvement:
....
....
....

Mark..........

LABORATORY REPORT MARKING SHEET

Course ——————————————————

Title ——————————————————

Report Sections	Guidelines	Max mark	Your mark	Comments
Introduction				
Method				
Results				
Discussion				
Conclusions				
General criteria				
Accuracy				
Presentation				

Total | 100 |

Overall comments

——————————————————————

——————————————————————

——————————————————————

University of the West of England
Certificate in Counselling Skills
****

CO-COUNSELLING ASSIGNMENT
FEEDBACK FROM SUE TO ....

Criterion 1: Evidence of personal development

Criterion 2: Evidence of understanding, insights,
willingness to explore and experiment

Criterion 3: Evidence of the ability to use
co-counselling creatively

Criterion 4: Clear communication

Result ....

DASS Psychology Programme: Assignment Attachment Sheet	Year 1	
	Year 2	

Name	Date in	Date back	Mark

Marking tutor	Personal tutor

WRITER'S SPECIFIC REQUESTS FOR FEEDBACK

MARKER'S GENERAL VIEW OF THE WORK

RATING SCALE	++	+	?	-	- -
INTRODUCTION TO THE ESSAY Interpretation of title and introduction	......	......	.....	.....	.....
DEVELOPMENT OF THE ESSAY					
Logical development	......	......	.....	.....	.....
Insight and originality	......	......	.....	.....	.....
Subject relevance	......	......	.....	.....	.....
Use of sources	......	......	.....	.....	.....
Use of evidence	......	......	.....	.....	.....
Understanding of topic	......	......	.....	.....	.....
Constructive critical analysis	......	......	.....	.....	.....
CONCLUSION TO THE ESSAY	......	......	.....	.....	.....
OTHER FEATURES					
Awareness of anti-discriminatory issues	......	......	.....	.....	.....
Relevance to social work practice	......	......	.....	.....	.....
Use of relevant personal experience	......	......	.....	.....	.....
Clarity of expression	......	......	.....	.....	.....
Spelling	......	......	.....	.....	.....
Presentation of references	......	......	.....	.....	.....

SPECIFIC ASPECTS OF YOUR ESSAY ....that the marker likes	SPECIFIC ASPECTS OF YOUR ESSAY ....that need more work

jthDASS.9/93

Chapter 10
Involving students in the assessment process

Students set the assignment titles   **43**

Students generally spend far more time answering questions than asking them, which is a pity, given that formulating questions is an invaluable aid to learning. If you give your students the opportunity to devise their own assignment titles, this will encourage them to relate to their course in a deeper and more challenging way. They will also be more motivated and so be likely to produce better assignments if they are writing on topics which they have chosen themselves.

A variety of ways of achieving this is suggested here. The suggestions range from those where the tutor retains some control to those where the students have full independence. You can of course use different methods on different occasions.

Individual students with tutor
Students are asked to devise their own essay titles in consultation with their tutor. This gives them the opportunity to choose their own topic but with guidance from the tutor on the wording of the question. This is the method which requires most tutor time.

Student group with tutor
Students are invited to submit suggestions for assignment titles. (If they need encouragement, you could help them to generate ideas by running a brainstorm exercise in a seminar slot.) The titles are considered for inclusion on the assignment list by a panel of staff and students. The benefits of this method are that students share their ideas and the assignment list, being the work of many hands, is very rich.

Individual student and group
Students are asked to devise their own essay titles in consultation with their seminar group. (This can be with or without the tutor present.) The benefits of this method are that students share their ideas and also receive

individual feedback: with a group whose members have learned to trust one another it works very well.

Individual student
Here students have total freedom to do what they like. There are no restrictions on them but on the other hand they receive no support. This method encourages autonomy in students but runs the risk of causing them feelings of isolation.

You can involve students further in the process by getting them to negotiate the due dates for the assignments and maybe also the criteria for extensions. You could even appoint a panel of staff and students with responsibility for considering requests for extensions.

Students negotiate the criteria   **44**

If criteria for assessment exist in any explicit form they are normally fixed by teaching staff. A useful alternative is for students to negotiate their own criteria with one another and with their tutor. This ensures not only that they know what the criteria are, but also that they understand and endorse them. It also gives them the opportunity to make their own proposals about assessment.

There are various ways in which you can enable your students to negotiate criteria with one another.

Unstructured discussion
If they are used to taking responsibility for their own learning it may be enough just to say to them 'I suggest that you propose your own criteria for assessing the next assignment. What I'll do is allow half an hour at the end of this session for you to discuss assessment and draw up a list of criteria'. You may like to stay and observe their discussion so that you understand the thinking behind their conclusions or you may feel that they will work better if you leave them on their own.

Structured discussion
If your students need a structured activity you can suggest that they all note down individually the characteristics of 'the best essay I ever wrote' or that they get into groups and note down the characteristics of 'the perfect essay'. These notes can then form the basis for the discussion of criteria.

Sentence completion
Alternatively, you can give them each a copy of the following handout and ask them to complete the sentences. They can then compare notes in small groups and each group can put forward proposals for criteria.

Criteria for assessment

Complete the following sentences
1   I would like to be given credit for ...
2   I would like not to be penalised for ...
3   I think people should be penalised for ...
4   I think that the essays which get the best marks should be the ones which ...
5   I think that the essays which get the worst marks should be the ones which ...

Inference
Another method is to start from criteria which are already in operation. For this each student will need to have a piece of work which you have marked. They analyse the feedback and grade that you have given them and infer what criteria you used. Or students in pairs can read each other's essays and give each other feedback from which the criteria are inferred. The group then decides whether these are criteria that they are happy with or whether they can improve on them.

Chaired discussion
If the students are not used to taking responsibility for their own learning, they may need you to chair a follow-up discussion before they can agree on their criteria.

Once they have a clear set of criteria they can proceed to negotiating with you. There are various ways of approaching this.

Accept the students' criteria
You may want to accept the students' criteria, as a matter of principle, from the start. This could be because their criteria are likely to be good and you

want to show them that you have confidence in their capabilities. Or it could be because the criteria are likely to be flawed and you want the students to learn from this. This would apply particularly in a situation where students are to produce a series of assignments and are encouraged to re-negotiate the criteria for each piece of work.

Challenge the students' criteria

If you want to encourage students to see the flaws in their criteria, you can play a challenging role and ask questions of the type 'What do you mean by .. ?' or 'How do you justify .. ?' or 'Why did you include .. ?' or 'What if .. ?' The outcome of this method is an amended version of the students' criteria.

Show the students your own criteria

This is the method which leaves most control in the hands of the tutor. Show the students your own criteria and ask them to make comments, criticisms and suggestions based on their own discussions. The outcome of this method is an amended version of the tutor's criteria.

Whatever method you and your students use to arrive at their criteria, you need to ensure that they end up with a clear list which everyone understands and agrees to.

Introducing peer assessment   45

Many tutors are reluctant to introduce peer assessment in their classes, in spite of its potential for the development of students' autonomy, maturity and critical abilities. Such reluctance seems to be based on fears that the results may be unreliable or the students resentful or the experience chaotic. All of these are of course potential hazards but they can be reduced or even avoided by careful implementation of the following principles.

Start it early
Students arriving at university generally have few preconceptions about assessment; they will be open-minded about any method you present to them. It is a good idea to start peer assessment in the first term, before they are set in their ways.

Another reason for starting early is that on most degree courses first year marks do not contribute towards the students' final results. This should mean that they will be more willing to try peer assessment.

Start it small
If you introduce peer assessment as just one element of the assessment or weight it so that it does not count for much (see item 50), students will not feel that they are taking too great a risk. Alternatively, you can ask them to begin by giving one another feedback rather than marks or even solely positive feedback.

Make it easy
Start with simple pieces of assessment which have clear marking criteria (see chapter 8) or preferably a marking scheme for students to follow (see item 34). This will make the results more reliable.

Make it clear
Give students a very clear statement of your rationale for peer assessment

and the procedure which they are to follow (see item 46). Get them to agree to the procedure and then insist that they stick to it. This will ensure that things run smoothly.

Rehearse it
You can get students to do a practice peer assessment exercise which does not count towards their year's result or you can check all their grades the first time they do the exercise and give them feedback about standards etc.

Make it rewarding
Praise students for their achievements.

Use anonymity
If students use numbers instead of their names on their written assignments, they feel less exposed when doing a peer assessment exercise. They are also reassured because it is more likely to be fair (see item 53).

Structuring a peer assessment exercise   46

It may be quicker to run a peer assessment exercise than to mark a set of assignments yourself but it is much more complex: you are dealing with a large number of markers all of whom are relative beginners. Aspects of the assessment process which are normally left implicit need to be made explicit.

The structuring of a peer assessment exercise is described here in terms of the stages of the procedure.

a   Briefing the students
First detail the procedure which students are to follow, including the time allocated for each stage. These instructions should be presented on a handout or overhead projector or whiteboard. Then encourage students to ask questions so that they can clarify details and reassure themselves.

b   Agreeing criteria
Remind students of the assessment criteria which have been agreed and/or explain the marking scheme which they are to use. Give them copies of all such paperwork.

c   Organising the marking
Each script needs to be marked by several students so scripts have to be rotated. This can be done in groups of any size. Small sub-groups allow more discussion among the markers but cause delays while students wait for one another to finish reading. A large group runs more smoothly because students' different reading speeds are not a problem. Just stack the assignments in one place and get students to take one, mark it, replace it, take another and so on.

The length of time required for this will depend on the length and complexity of the assignments and the experience of the students. You could, as an alternative to setting a time limit, decide to call a halt to this stage of the procedure when all scripts have been marked by at least three students.

d   Introducing safeguards
If you want students to do their marking without seeing the marks which other students have given, you will need to attach an envelope to each script, into which students place their marks and comments.

If assignments are anonymous and you want to prevent students from marking their own, you can divide the student group in two and get one half of the group to mark the assignments of the other half.

e   Agreeing the marks
There are many ways in which students can agree their marks. You can make a choice of method on the basis of how much autonomy you want students to have. Or you can invite them to choose. A list of alternative methods is given here.

- Give each assignment the average of the marks awarded to it by the students.

- Give each assignment the average of the marks awarded to it by the students unless there are differences of degree classification between markers or the spread is more than a certain percentage. In such cases you can act as arbiter or a panel of students can be appointed to make the final decisions.

- Mark the assignments yourself and combine your marks with the average marks given by the students according to an agreed weighting.

- Accept the students' marks relative to one another but adjust the whole set up or down if they are too low or too high compared with departmental norms.

The amount of time needed for this stage of the process will depend on which option you and your students choose.

f   Reviewing the experience
It is crucial that students are given the opportunity to reflect on the exercise, identify problems and suggest ways in which they could be solved. If you make a note of these and implement them, the exercise will run even more smoothly next time.

Allow at least half an hour for this stage of the process. If students are reluctant to speak up in a large group, get them to discuss the exercise in sub-groups and report back.

Peer assessment of seminar presentations   47

Seminars lend themselves particularly well to peer assessment. Whenever students present seminar papers they are in fact subject to informal evaluation by their peers. If student seminar presentations are already a part of your teaching programme, you will find it easy to formalise this evaluation and develop it into a peer assessment exercise. You will also find that running the exercise will take very little extra time.

This item offers an account of a real case of a seminar group where the students assessed one another's presentations using a marking scheme which they devised themselves. The students were in their first year of a degree course, BSc (Hons) Nursing at the University of the West of England. (On this course, first year marks do not contribute to the final result.) This case illustrates the principles outlined in the two preceding items. For ease of comparison, the subheadings used are the same as those in item 46.

a   Briefing the students
This was the students' first experience of peer assessment so their tutor was careful to offer them a full rationale for the method and lots of reassurance. He also gave them a detailed account of the stages of the procedure.

b   Agreeing criteria (see also item 44)
The students devised their own marking scheme. The first stage was a brainstorm: students called out suggestions for criteria, which the tutor wrote on the board. They then discussed their suggestions and by collapsing some, modifying some and dropping others they arrived at an agreed list of criteria. Next they rated the criteria and apportioned marks to them. The tutor chaired the discussion but withheld his own views; he did this in order to validate the students and demonstrate to them that this was something they could do without his help.

The marking scheme which the students devised is reproduced below.

c   Organising the marking
Students were each given a copy of the marking scheme for each seminar presentation. They filled them in and totalled their marks. The sheets were collected each time by one member of the group who calculated the overall mark.

d   Introducing safeguards
The students filled in the marking sheets on the spot and were not permitted to take them away. This prevented any possible loss of sheets, delay in collating results or collusion among students.

e   Agreeing the marks
The students agreed to take the average of their marks as the group's mark. At this stage, however, they did not have the confidence to let this mark stand alone. They negotiated with the tutor that he would also assess each student, using the students' criteria, and that his marks would carry equal weight with theirs.

f   Reviewing the experience
It was clear to the students that their marking scheme was not ideal and would need to be modified for the next exercise. They concentrated on this in their review.

Peer assessment of seminar presentation

Criteria for peer assessment of seminar presentation devised by first year BSc (Hons) Nursing students.
Teacher awards 50%, and students award 50% of the marks.

		Possible total	*Your mark*
1	Use of AV aids & other teaching methods	20%	....
2	Timing	10%	....
3	Interaction between students & interest	20%	....
4	Structure of seminar } Style of presentation } Understandability } 6 x 5% = 30% Logical sequence of ideas } Clarity of speech } Lack of distracting mannerisms }		....
5	Appropriate educational level for group and well-referenced	20%	....
	Total	100% / 2 =	____

Student-directed self and peer assessment 48

When engaging in self and peer assessment, some groups of students need the kind of guidance from their tutors that is described in, for example, items 24, 45 and 46 of this book. Other groups are fully capable of directing their own self and peer assessment activities. A competent group is likely to have some or all of the following characteristics.

- The group has had experience of doing self and peer assessment under the guidance of a tutor.

- The students are mature, emotionally if not necessarily chronologically.

- The students have been taught as a group for some time and are used to giving one another support and constructive criticism.

- The students have done some group work as part of their course.

- The students' assessed work is presented publicly. This work could be, for example, assessed seminar presentations, exhibitions (see item 22), or interpersonal skills.

The example described here is the real case of a group of students on a one-year part-time certificate in counselling skills at the University of the West of England. The group had all the characteristics listed above. (Their assessed work was presented publicly in the sense that every teaching session included a practical period in which students practised their counselling skills with one another.)

The self assessment and the peer assessment were two assessment elements which counted equally with the other, tutor-assessed, elements: students needed to pass all of these in order to pass the course.

The group was allowed nine hours over three weeks towards the end of the course for the self and peer assessment.

Students were given copies of the handout reproduced opposite. This was needed so that they would be clear about the task, the programme and the role of the tutors and also, paradoxically, so that they would realise how much freedom they had.

The outcome was that the students completed the task in the time allocated without needing to consult the tutors. They had the courage to refer some of their number who were not yet ready to pass. And, most importantly, they said they had learned a lot in taking on such a difficult and rewarding challenge.

UNIVERSITY OF THE WEST OF ENGLAND
CERTIFICATE IN COUNSELLING SKILLS
SELF AND PEER ASSESSMENT

The task
For the self and peer element of this course you are expected:
a   to give feedback to yourself and others on your skills, abilities and potential as counsellors (this can be based on your observation of a counselling session and/or anything relevant you have noticed about the person in the group or elsewhere)
b   to assess yourselves and others as counsellors on a pass/referred basis.

Taking the task seriously
Remember that you have a responsibility only to pass group members who you are confident about. It is better that people who, in your personal opinion, are not good enough should be referred at this stage and given the chance to improve.

Doing the self and peer assessment
You can do this in any agreed way you like as long as the available time is shared fairly.
Agree criteria or not as you prefer.
Take coffee breaks when you like and take time for review, relaxation or games if you want.

The programme
Three sessions have been set aside for the self, peer and course assessment.
Please give the course leader a list of results of the self and peer assessment by 8.30pm on 27 June.
Please allow the half hour between 8.30 and 9.00 on 27 June for the course assessment. As many of the tutors as are able will join you for this.

The role of the tutors
Tutors will be available on 13, 20 and 27 June. We will be happy to give advice, information, support etc., if asked. You can invite us to join the group or consult us in Room 10.

Chapter 11
Issues in assessment

Choosing assessment methods 49

Generally speaking, student learning is assessment-driven: students put most of their effort into aspects of their course which are assessed, particularly latterly when there has been more competition for jobs. This means that the choices you make about assessment will largely determine what your students learn. So it follows that, before you decide how your students are to be assessed, you need to decide what they are to learn (knowledge, abilities, skills etc.) and why they are to learn it (for its own sake, to get a job, to learn how to learn etc.) Then you are ready to choose your assessment methods. This is straightforward if you remember what different assessment methods offer, for example:

- Essays (see chapter 1) test whether students can sustain a leisurely argument in continuous prose.

- Multiple choice questions (see chapter 2) generally test students' knowledge. They can also test their skills in reasoning, deduction etc.

- Exams and other timed tests (see chapter 4) assess students' ability to memorise and their ability to respond to a challenge in a controlled situation. They also offer more safeguards against cheating than other methods of assessment.

- Projects (see chapter 7) test students' ability to take individual responsibility for a sustained piece of practical work.

A further decision to be made is the extent to which students will share in the assessment process (see chapter 10).

A principle of assessment, which could contribute to your decision-making, is that the more data you have from different sources, the better the profile you have of the student.

Constraints on staff need to be taken into account too. You may be restrained by professional bodies who specify particular methods of assessment for your students, often as a safeguard against cheating. It is, however, often possible to gain permission from such bodies to introduce a mixed assessment diet as long as a minimum number of the elements are formally examined.

Another constraint is time. However you may favour long essays as a method of assessment there will probably come a time when you and your colleagues are unable to cope with the marking. Then you will need to allow pragmatism to affect your choice of assessment methods and use self and peer assessment (see items 45-48) or exams (see chapter 4) or computed-marked multiple choice questions (see item 11).

The assessment regime can of course be used creatively to achieve different aims in different years. For example by astute selection of methods you can teach students how to learn in year 1, test their knowledge in year 2 and get them to demonstrate their abilities in year 3.

Weighting marks   50

Weighting marks so that they count for different proportions of a student's overall result is an aspect of assessment which has developed rapidly since institutions of higher education started storing marks on computer. It is now an easy task to fine-tune the assessment to cater for different student groups and to reflect the requirements of particular parts of a course.

The computer can easily deal with complicated formulae. As long as you are clear about what you want, you can devise a programme to meet your needs. You could even weight a module in the proportions 3.8% / 21% / 75.2% if it suited your purpose.

Weighting marks allows staff to make implicit statements about variety, emphasis, balance and restrictions. Some examples of weighting in action are given here.

Allowing variety
Different modules or parts of a course can be weighted differently. For example,

	Coursework		*Exam*
	Report	Essay	
Module 1	25%	25%	50%
Module 2	10%	20%	70%
Module 3	35%	45%	20%

Showing progression

If you want to give students more credit for their final year work, you can give it more weight. You could, for example, weight the second and third year marks in the proportion 40 /60 or give a dissertation mark twice the weighting of the other marks.

Preventing cheating

You may want to include an exam as a safeguard against cheating but be reluctant to devote very many marks to it. In this case you could give it a weighting of, say, 10% but also require students to pass it.

Setting diagnostic essays

Not many students will do a diagnostic essay which does not contribute towards their overall mark. You can, however, set a diagnostic essay with a weighting of 5% which will encourage students to do it but will not penalise those who do it badly.

Declassified degrees 51

Classified degrees are unknown on the Continent and in the United States. They are a manifestation of the British social class system, enabling tutors to categorise a student as 'a first class mind', 'a classic 2.2' or even a third class person.

They are also unjust in that the process for deciding on the class varies between institutions: some base it on a strict average of final marks, others operate the kind of averaging where very high or very low marks are allowed to skew the result, others again weight some marks more than others or alternatively compute only a proportion of the marks or base the class decision on the median mark.

In addition, every institution has its own regulations - or case law, or whims - on which to base decisions for raising students across the borderlines. Recent research (see item 53) indicates that in disputed cases men students' marks are more likely to be raised than women students'.

The following list of component marks of a student's final degree result is used to demonstrate some of these discrepancies.

	Year 2		Year 3
Module 1	40%	Module 1	63%
Module 2	50%	Module 2	66%
Module 3	52%	Module 3	62%
Module 4	55%	Dissertation	75%

- A strict average of these marks gives a result of 57.875%, which is a 2.2.

- In a system where the second and third year marks are weighted in the ratio 40/60, the result is 59.6%. This gives a 2.1 or 2.2 classification, depending on the examiners' policy (and practice) on borderline marks: whether, for example, they round up decimals above 0.5.

- If the final mark is based on the best seven marks out of the eight, the result is 60.43%, which is a clear 2.1.

- If staff are encouraged to 'use the whole range of marks' and the dissertation is given a mark of 85%, this in combination with the 40/60 weighting will also give a clear 2.1 mark (61.1%).

- If the lowest mark is dropped and the classification is based on the median mark (63%), this gives a higher 2.1 mark.

- A combination of a dissertation mark of 85%, the weighting of the dissertation as 25% of the total and the dropping of the lowest mark will give 64.75%: a 'good' 2.1 (in a system where rounding up applies).

An alternative to a classified degree is the transcript. This consists of a list for each student of the modules or component parts of the award with a mark for each. In addition it can provide a record of anything else which the student has achieved, such as wordprocessing skills, prizes, positions of responsibility etc. A note indicating any extenuating circumstances can be added. A transcript of this kind gives a potential employer or admissions tutor a profile of the student which provides much more useful information than a degree classification.

Producing transcripts is not an onerous task. On a modular course - or any course with discrete assessed elements - where marks are stored on the computer, the data for the transcript already exist; they just need to be printed out for each student. The transcript for the student whose marks are given above is shown opposite.

The University of Quality Assurance
Faculty of Humanities Transcript
BA (Hons) in Geographical Studies

A. Student
1989-1993

Year 1

H1CC05	Computing and the Humanities	78%
H1CC01	Introduction to Cultural Studies	60%
H1CG01	Changing Human Geography of the United Kingdom	65%
H1CG02	Environmental Issues	65%

Year 2

L2CF01	French	40%
H2CG22	Changing Natural and Physical Environments	50%
H3CG23	Urban Geography and Planning	52%
H3CG25	The Geography of Leisure and Tourism	55%

Year 3

H3CG27	Human Impact on the Environment	63%
H3CG28	Geography of Global Development	66%
H3CG29	Wildlife Conservation: Principle and Practice	62%
H3CG90	Dissertation in Geographical Studies	75%

'More roads, less speed: planning the transport infrastructure'

Unassessed activities

Student representative, Course Management Committee, 1990-1
Attendance at University Co-counselling Training Course (32 hours),
March 1991
Student Union Welfare Officer (Sabbatical Post), 1991-2
Student Administrator, Geography Field Week, February 1993

Signed: ....
Designation: ....
Date: ....

Pass/fail assessment   **52**

A pass/fail course is one where there is no grading or differentiation among those students who pass, but only between those who pass and those who fail. A pass/fail decision is also generally the outcome of criterion-referenced assessment (see item 38) but for different reasons. The main purpose of criterion-referenced assessment is to ensure that students who successfully complete a course can do a particular range of things competently; pass/fail courses are usually designed to avoid the negative side effects of assessment rather than to establish performance standards. Such negative side effects can include competitiveness between students, student preoccupation with assessment rather than with learning, student anxiety about performance, and a heavy workload for tutors.

Pass/fail assessment is usually introduced onto those courses where it is felt to be especially important for students to explore the subject matter in an open and flexible way without fear of the consequences, and where there are few 'right' answers or defined skills, and few clear performance criteria. Passing is usually defined in terms of fulfilling minimum criteria such as: attendance at classes; submitting assignments; completing a self-assessment form or presenting a seminar paper.

Pass/fail courses are quite common in the context of modular or credit accumulation courses where individual short units count towards a final qualification, such as a degree. The assessment pressure in such courses can be relentless and pass/fail units are introduced in order to allow students some time to relax and learn for the sake of learning without jeopardising their overall average marks.

Pass/fail elements can also be built in as components of otherwise conventionally assessed courses. Regulations can be framed in the form: 'Students must gain an average of 40% on coursework and the exam *and submit a project'*. This can encourage a more adventurous, creative, and therefore risky, approach to the project work than might be the case if it was marked in the same way as other course elements.

On many degree courses it is considered sufficient for students to pass the first year exams in order to progress to the second year: the first year marks do not contribute to the final degree result. This situation lends itself to the introduction of pass/fail elements in the first year or even a first year which is assessed entirely on a pass/fail basis. This gives students more freedom to experiment and take risks and gives non-standard entry students a chance to catch up with their peers. It also relieves staff of much of their marking.

Gender bias   53

Research indicates that examiners in higher education are more likely to award firsts or thirds to men and 2.2 degrees to women. This is irrespective of the gender of the marker. These differences, which are in keeping with British society's view of men as extreme and women as mediocre, do not occur on courses where students write their papers anonymously [1].

If you and your colleagues want to institute anonymous marking, this is one procedure.

a   Each student is allocated a number. This can be done by an administrator or another member of staff not directly involved in assessing students.

b   Students write their numbers on all their scripts.

c   Staff submit lists of student numbers, together with marks, to the administrator, who computes the marks.

d   The student numbers are translated back into names only when all the results and degree classifications have been agreed.

If students' coursework is marked anonymously you may find yourself in situations such as one-to-one tutorials where students need to identify themselves as the authors of their assignments in order to be able to discuss their work with you. The danger here is that you will recognise future pieces of their work. You can, however, easily avert this by making it a condition of attending tutorials that students type their scripts.

Reference
[1]   Clare Bradley, 'Sex Bias in Student Assessment Overlooked?' in *Assessment and Evaluation in Higher Education,* Vol. 18, No. 1, 1993.

Alphabetical list of contents